David Chaplin

# Can
# Do
# Better

novum pro

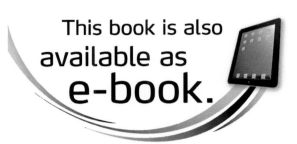

This book is also
available as
e-book.

www.novum-publishing.co.uk

ISBN 978-3-99146-161-6
Editing: Philip Kelly
Cover photos:
Vladimir Ceresnak I Dreamstime.com;
David Chaplin
Cover design, layout & typesetting:
novum publishing
Internal illustrations: David Chaplin

The images provided by the author
have been printed in the highest
possible quality.

**www.novum-publishing.co.uk**

# Contents

# Preface

As a Headmaster, or indeed a former Headmaster, it is important to maintain one's dignity. It is essential at all costs to avoid being laughed at. George Orwell had the same problem when he was working as a sub-divisional policeman in Burma, and it drove him to shooting an elephant.

There is a widely held assumption that headmasters must be clever and knowledgeable, an assumption which in my case is entirely misplaced.

Years ago, I took our dog to the vets. Medicine was prescribed, a cheque duly completed and I sat in the packed waiting room whilst the receipt was prepared. Imagine my horror when the vet came dancing into the waiting room, waving the cheque in the air and shouting with glee, "He's a Headmaster and he can't spell veterinary."

To some extent the fear of exposure has haunted me all my life, so it was very challenging in later years when I kept finding myself caught short in places where there were no decent options for dealing with the problem, not even a convenient bush! The situation was so acute that I was reduced to seeing the doctor.

I explained the problem. He was inclined to shrug it off. "We're old men, David! What else can you expect?"

When it came to the examination, upon which I insisted, I could understand why he had been so reluctant to undertake further investigation.

He removed his gloved hand, and I could tell from his expression that all was not well. This was undoubtedly prostate cancer.

Various procedures followed including a biopsy carried out by a locum who seemed to take an unreasonable delight in the seriousness of the diagnosis. "Goodness me, Mr Chaplin, this is very bad! Oh dear, this is very bad indeed!"

In the event I was passed on to a truly wonderful oncologist who has managed to keep me alive and well for over ten years with a clever combination of drugs and radiotherapy.

For all that, it has been difficult not to be drawn into thinking about one's own mortality, to take stock, especially when friends and relations around you are falling prey to illness.

I know without question what has mattered to me most in my life – my wife and family.

But what of the rest of it ...

# Chapter 1

# Early Days

It was not an auspicious beginning. I was born the youngest of six children, undoubtedly the runt of the litter. As soon as I was old enough to be called names I was known as Spindles. I was almost certainly a mistake, but my mother doted on me and spoilt me. Consequently, my father disliked me. This was entirely understandable. Apart from anything else, I was an annoying child. His dislike mainly manifested itself in his behaving as though I didn't exist, but there were moments of more pointed cruelty which he would pass off as jokes. One of these was to forget, "accidentally", to serve me at the meal table. I found this hard to handle and usually ran out of the room in tears.

Occasionally he would wallop me, much to my mother's dismay. My sister tells me that once it was because I put a peg on my nose, which seems a little harsh. Perhaps he was just a little too old and irritable to cope with a young child.

In those days there was a popular cartoon series called the *Gambols* which portrayed the daily life of a chaotic family. It is fair to say that our home life was gambolic. Our address was number 32 Park Lane, but this was Norwich, not London, and our house was altogether less grand than the address might have led you to believe. It was a relatively small house for eight people, and we lived somewhat on top of each other.

We had a dog called Clover who used to eat coal and chase her tail furiously round the kitchen.

There was what might loosely be described as a conservatory. This was impenetrable as it was full of junk and numerous piles of back numbers of *Punch* and the *National Geographic* which no-one appeared to have read.

Furniture and fittings were basic. My parents did not feel the need for lampshades, bookshelves, curtains or carpets. The only water heater we had was a geyser in the bathroom, and this regularly threatened to explode. All the laundry went through the mangle on Monday morning.

The front garden consisted of gravel and weeds and the back garden was what an estate agent might have described as "mature". It was an uncultivated mess. However, it boasted a splendid chestnut tree in which we were able make camps and from which we could throw rotten plums at Mr Woodcock's combinations which hung on the line in the neighbouring garden.

There were two standard punishments: "Dire Disgrace" confined you to your bedroom for a couple of hours, and "Durance Vile" to the cellar. In fairness to my parents, the second of these was generally issued as a threat and was rarely implemented, not even when Mrs Woodcock complained about the state of her husband's underwear.

We had a wireless and my father liked to listen to *The Archers* each evening. During this fifteen-minute period silence was required. My youngest sister was (and still is) very talkative and found this difficult. My father once broke a plate over her head for interrupting the everyday story of countryfolk.

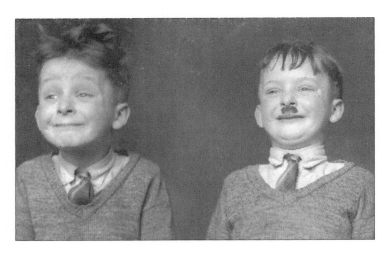

From an early age I liked dressing up. From time to time, I would don a white wigwam and preach to my youngest sister and her dolls from halfway up the stairs. I also did a passable imitation of Laurel and Hardy who were popular then.

Park Lane had a life of its own. On the other side from the elderly Woodcocks were the Clarks. They had three children. Karen, the eldest, was a large girl who used to canter round the garden pretending to be a horse, making whooping noises and whipping her thighs. I liked to watch her through a crack in the fence.

The Winters lived beyond the Woodcocks. Mary Winter was very beautiful in a wistful sort of way. The other Mary, Mary Hill, lived at the end of the lane. She was loud, red-haired and naughty.

There were two ladies on the lane who were mad. One, a Miss Legotty, used to push an empty pushchair up and down the street singing hymns and the other, Mrs Daniel, used to enter her house (number 10) not through the door but rather by climbing through the front window. Rumour had it that all the furniture in her house was upside down, but I am not sure that this was ever verified.

Opposite our house was Denbigh Hill which boasted six shops, a pub and a brothel. There was also a fishmongers which was run by a man who I like to think was called Mr Pilchard, although I have a feeling his real name was Punchard. He was very slow and red in the face on account of his predilection for alcohol. Occasionally he used to take me on his rounds in the back of his van with the fish. My parents ought to have worried about this on a number of counts. Perhaps they never knew about it, although I must have smelt fishy on my return.

Most years we had a family holiday, but never outside Norfolk. One year we stayed in a cottage in Bunwell and were tasked to look after the hens. Despite his addiction to *The Archers*, my dad was not a countryman. Each day a few of the hens died, so that by the time of our departure after two weeks there was none left. This cast a shadow over the holiday. It did not lighten the mood that my elder brother very nearly drowned attempting to cross the pond in a metal oil drum.

For several years in succession, we stayed at Henstead Farm. This was run by a Polish opera singer called Mr Vaskovitch. He used to sing *Nessun Dorma* as he milked the cows, which they seemed to enjoy, but much of the farm was run down and derelict. Mrs Vaskovitch had a shrill voice, and I can still hear her calling for Andre, their little boy. Andre always seemed to be missing. I have happy memories of running free on the farm.

My mother was called Ethel and was affectionately known as Eth. She was born in Scarborough and her father ran a draper's shop there. He had died long before I was born but I knew from my mother that he was a kind and gentle man. This is borne out by the few sepia photographs we have of him. His favourite pastime was fly-fishing. I would have loved to have known him.

My mother studied at Scarborough School of Art: she was a very skilled water colourist and calligrapher, producing a series of landscapes, illuminated texts and Christmas cards that were a great delight for her family and friends. I felt she was her happiest when she was painting: she used to half whistle little tunes.

Mum devoted her entire life to the care of her house, her husband and her children. Like her father, she was kind and gentle, but was also inclined to worry and fret. She did not socialise much, and as the children left home, she became increasingly frustrated by the emptiness and narrowness of her life.

Mum enjoyed reading and was particularly devoted to the writings of the famous Methodist preacher, Dr Leslie Weatherhead.

My eldest sister was much like her mum and suffered from nerves to the extent that for quite some time she was unable to face going to school. My youngest sister, the chatty one, had a similar, if much briefer, period of school phobia, but it is likely that this was copycat behaviour because she did not seem to lack confidence. In fact, she was quite forthright, and I remember her exacting terrible punishments on her dolls. My middle sister was the happy-go-lucky one, although she always claims that she was neglected because of being in the middle.

My father was a frustrated artist. He was an immensely gifted craftsman working in a wide range of materials, and he had a vivid, if slightly macabre, imagination. His father had started his working life as a glass blower, but later did better for himself and his family by becoming an insurance superintendent. He was said to be a stern and strict man who expected to be obeyed by his children. He felt that his son would never earn a decent living as an artist so insisted that he study architecture. Dad did as he was told.

He had been born and bred in Yorkshire but he was forced to move to Norwich in the recession in the mid-Thirties to find work. Here he prospered and was able to set up his own practice. He came to specialise in cheap housing and crematoria, the first possibly leading to the second. I suppose he earned a good living, but he was not a big spender: his only indulgence was fast cars. At one stage he had a TR2 which was racing green and made a lot of noise.

Dad made considerable sacrifices to see all six of his children through private school, the three boys boarding from the age of thirteen. I suspect he was especially pleased to see me off to boarding school.

# Chapter 2

# School

I am grateful to my father for his generosity although in my case I do not think he had good value from his investment as I do not think I benefited much from the schooling. I was smart enough to get by, but not remotely academic. Not that the schools did much to fire the imagination, to stimulate intellectual curiosity and a love of learning.

The masters at my prep school were an odd collection: Colonel W taught history and was so old that he was said to be the only teacher in the country on a war pension as a result of a wound from a bow and arrow; Mr S was bearded and taught English. Rumour had it that he used to beat his stepdaughter with a belt – I find this unlikely now as he was, in my experience, a remarkably mild and gentle man; Mr W taught Latin and was so energetic that he spat when he spoke. We kept our distance. Mr J taught French, I think, and had a lime green Riley 1.5 which I rather admired. He used to take me on my own to Snetterton motor racing some weekends. I have disliked motor-racing ever since.

Finally, there was a bearded maths teacher whose name I have forgotten. He used to throw the board duster at us from time to time for no obvious reason. This was good for our reflexes. He had also devised a punishment of quite extraordinary ingenuity. The offender was required to bend down with his head below the mantelpiece in the classroom. He then had to stick his hands out in front of his body and the teacher would dangle a ruler just above them. To bring the punishment to an end you had to catch the ruler just as it was released. This was made more difficult as the teacher would whack your bottom simultaneously with the release of the ruler, causing you to miss the ruler and bang your head on the mantelpiece above.

I don't remember any lady teachers.

The headmaster was an austere and distant figure whom I only ever met over a good caning. One of my more vivid recollections is standing outside his door, feeling very small and waiting to be summoned. This happened several times and the odd thing was that I never really understood what I had done wrong.

The other punishment which I incurred with remarkable regularity was the Labour Squad. This involved raking up leaves in the headmaster's garden on a Saturday morning for a couple of hours and would doubtless provoke outrage were it to be implemented now. I don't think it did me any harm: as a matter of fact, I have developed rather a liking for gardening.

I suppose it was about a mile from home to school and from an early age I would cycle. I even cycled home for lunch each day. I remember cycling into the back of a car once and discovering when I got home that the bicycle had broken in two. This upset me considerably, but not as much as it upset my father.

I became very familiar with the ride, but I still remember becoming hopelessly lost in the smog. It was so dense that a bus could only move if someone walked a yard or so in front to check that the way was clear.

My early schooldays were not particularly happy, but nor were they traumatic. We began most days by marching in platoons round the schoolyard. I am not sure why we did this, but I quite enjoyed being deliberately out of step. Bullying was common. There was a boy called de Jong, who was nicknamed Pongo Jongo and who was hunted during morning break. Golding had it right, I am afraid. Conveniently, I cannot remember whether I joined in or not. Most of my memories of the school are hazy.

I think I might have been teased a bit myself. Being the youngest child, I was mainly clothed and kitted out with hand-me-downs. My sisters all attended the Norwich High School where the uniform was a sickly green. Remarkably, it seems they even insisted on green knickers. Sadly, I inherited several pairs. When changing for games the other boys pointed at me with glee and exclaimed, "Those are knickers! He's got green knickers on!" This was followed by peals of gleeful laughter. Limply I would insist they were not knickers, but I knew in my heart of hearts that they were.

We had boxing at school. Nobody taught us how to box: it was merely a question of hit or be hit. I think I was quite good at being hit.

My school reports have a distinctive theme. At the end of one term the Headmaster wrote: "I still expect him to do much better and I am proposing to put him on my personal report list for next term to find out why so many members of staff are dissatisfied with him."

From the reading of subsequent reports it appears that putting me on the "personal report list" failed to generate any improvement.

I was sent off to boarding school at the age of thirteen and here I was genuinely miserable. Being useless at sport at a boys-only school is a massive disadvantage and being a sickly child, I spent a lot of time in the sanatorium. At least there was female company there and a motherly matron.

My housemaster was a chain-smoking, bachelor musician who appeared to have no interest in the well-being of the boys under his care. I once asked him if I could go home for a weekend as it was my sister's birthday. He curled his lip, exhaled a mouthful of smoke, and declared, "You are a baby, Chaplin, aren't you? Grow up!" I supposed that meant no.

I lived in the shadow of my two brothers. The elder was the star of the family. He won the top scholarship to the boarding school, thus paving the way for his two brothers to follow, and subsequently read English at Cambridge. He went on to study architecture and then joined my father's practice. This possibly proved to be a mistake,

The younger brother made his mark at the school in a different way: he was a leading light in the combined cadet force. He was so important that on parade he marched ahead of the school band throwing a stick in the air. I think he might even have worn a bear skin. He also attracted admiration as an intrepid mountaineer.

I compared badly with both brothers, especially in my father's eyes.

Perversely, I disliked the CCF. I found the uniform prickly and the sergeant major who ran it unpleasant. He was a small man with a loud voice and false teeth. He had a joke. Just the one, which he would bellow on the parade ground. "When I was in Baghdad, you were in dad's bag." On one occasion he bellowed so loudly his teeth flew out.

I drew no inspiration from the teachers. There was one teacher who was kind to me, but I fear he had ulterior motives. He called me Chas – ridiculous – and wrote me long, intimate letters which I found embarrassing and hid.

Mr S taught German. Every lesson we took it in turns to read from the set book. Mr S was so lazy he had to ask us which page we were on at the beginning of each lesson. For all he knew we could have read the same pages from the book each lesson for the entire term. As a treat at the end of term we sang German songs. I can still give a passable rendering of *Die Lorelei*, so I suppose I learned something.

Tubby H taught chemistry and failed to make any impression on my complete ignorance of the subject. He liked giving out punishments. "Name," he would bellow out of the blue, but often in my direction.

"Chaplin."

"4Y."

This condemned me to getting up early on four consecutive mornings to write lines.

There was an entire alphabet of punishments: C's were for being late. T's were for having your hands in your pockets. Receive two of them in one week and your pockets were sewn up. As far as I recall there was no punishment for being unkind.

The school was a Methodist foundation, and we did a lot of chapel. The services did not make a great impression on me, but they were a welcome break from the unpleasantness of school life in general. Once, Mum's hero, Leslie Weatherhead, came to preach. He told the story of a little boy who refused to eat his prunes for tea. The parents tried every tactic they knew, but in the end resorted to, "If you don't eat your prunes, God will be angry!" Parents be warned, this never works.

That night there was a terrible storm, driving rain and alarming thunder and lightning. The parents went downstairs to unplug the television and check the windows. They were just about to return to bed when they were surprised to see their little boy pad downstairs. He went into the kitchen, opened the fridge door, took out the bowl of prunes and quietly worked his way through them. Once finished, he placed the bowl in the sink and set off to return to bed. As he passed his parents, he muttered, "A lot of fuss over a few prunes."

I can't remember the burden of the sermon, but I rather hope it was about God being merciful rather than judgemental.

The nearest I came to any sporting success at the school was to act as scorer for the first eleven. I think the attractions were travelling in the bus and enjoying the match teas, but these were mitigated by the fact that the eleven heroic sportsmen would have nothing to do with me. It was a lonely occupation, but I did come to enjoy the statistics.

I used to dread the games sessions when two captains were chosen from the boys and were allowed to pick their teams. Invariably I was the last to be chosen.

One of my escapes was acting: being someone other than myself was such a relief. Sadly, the one starring role I had at school succeeded in making things very much worse. Amazingly, given my appearance, I was cast as Cleopatra in Shakespeare's *Anthony and Cleopatra*. I remember applying the asp to my artificial bosom and thinking that it might be quite a blessing if it were the real thing applied to my actual chest. My father came to see the performance: it was the only occasion that he visited the school during my entire career there. His verdict was that the performance was hilarious and embarrassing in about equal measure.

These unhappy years are best glossed over but I can see that they put paid to the last shreds of confidence I might have had in myself. I became chronically shy and self-conscious. Meeting a stranger, or even talking to my elder brother, whom I did not know very well, caused me to turn bright red in the face.

To a certain extent I have grown out of this but, looking back on my childhood I am not surprised that as an adult I have always found it easier to relate with women than to relate with men, especially confident and hearty men. I was never clubbable, and never will be.

At the end of it all I achieved three modest A levels and qualified for Durham University. There I studied English during the day, mainly because there was nothing else to do, and drank Newcastle Brown in great quantities at night. I wasted my opportunities at university, and I regret that now.

Before Durham I had a gap year and, quite remarkably, I was appointed as a teaching assistant at the very prep school where I had led such a dubious career. It was a role for which I was wholly unqualified, but it was quite interesting seeing it all from a different perspective. It did not improve my impression of the school.

During this year I was able to develop my acting career at the Maddermarket theatre in Norwich. My first appearance was as a soldier in *Henry V*. I had a pike and in cheering us all "once more unto the breach" I managed to get this caught in one of the flats and demolished half the set.

Mercifully I was forgiven and awarded the part of the Miller's son in *Puss in Boots*. In this version, I was carried off by an ogre in a net. My four-year-old niece, who was in the audience, found this upsetting and very nearly brought the production to a halt with her wailing.

My final appearance was in a play called *Next Time I'll Sing to You*. It was a modern play which nobody understood, and on most nights the second half was played to an empty auditorium.

# Chapter 3

# Courtship and Marriage

From an early age I loved cars and driving. As a child I had a penny-farthing tricycle and I would spend hours pedalling up and down Park Lane pretending to be a bus, making engine noises and stopping at every other lamp post to collect imaginary passengers. I think a lot of the people on the street thought I was mad, like the lady with the pram. At one point I even transported my mother and her washing to the launderette on the back of the penny farthing.

Later, when I was a teenager and we had moved to a bigger house, my father allowed me to drive the Mini Countryman he kept as a runabout up and down our short drive. One of my sister's boyfriends was bewildered and surprised to be repeatedly prevented from turning into the drive by this mini which kept appearing at the gate only to disappear again.

We lived on the first floor of the house and the ground floor provided the rooms for the architectural practice. From time to time, I overheard my father dealing with the staff. He developed a bit of a stammer when he became cross which extended the length of the dressing down and made it all the more awful.

I like to think that my father grew to like me a little more as I grew up. Anyway, on my eighteenth birthday he generously gave me £500 to buy a green Morris Minor which I christened The Toad. It was quite cheap, even in those days, and the vehicle was not in mint condition. It was, therefore, a rash, not to say foolish, decision to drive it through Europe to Greece in the first long vac at university. It had to be Greece because one of the travelling friends was studying Classics and surprisingly qualified for a generous grant to visit the ancient ruins of Greece. This helped to fund the whole expedition.

Remarkably The Toad proved steady and reliable and the only travelling disaster resulted from my crass stupidity. At Thessalonica I decided to go swimming in the sea with the car key in the pocket of my trunks. It dropped out. We spent hours trawling up and down the beach to no avail. As dusk settled, we headed to the camp site in despair dropping into the café to ask whether by any chance someone had handed in a key. Miraculously someone had.

The other incident on the Grecian expedition marked the most important turning point in my entire life. We arrived in Tolon in the South Peloponnese and duly set up camp and settled down in our tents for a siesta.

An hour later sisters Sally and Mary Taylor arrived at the camp site in their brand new, bright red Mini Cooper S. They surveyed the scene, spotted the ancient Morris Minor and concluded that it would be safe to set up camp alongside it as it probably housed a couple of sensible grannies in tweeds and lace up shoes.

They were mistaken, as they discovered when we crawled out. Still, we struck up conversation and headed for the local taverna for a moussaka and a bottle of Sang d'Hercule.

To be honest I was rather taken with Sally but didn't have the nerve to say so or to ask for her address. The next morning, we bade farewell and the red mini shot off into the distance. I was left reflecting that I had just met the most attractive lady that it was possible to imagine.

We continued on our travels, taking in the sites at Delphi and Epidaurus, but the wonder of it all had gone just as the mini had disappeared into the distance.

Then a miracle occurred. We were trundling along a mountain road when I spotted a red dot in the rear-view mirror, and soon the girls were overtaking and flagging us down. Where were we camping, they wanted to know. Not because they sought our company but rather because they had run out of food and were aware that we still had a couple of tins of sardines. This time we did exchange addresses. I am bound to reflect here that if I had not met and re-met Sally my life would have been very different and almost certainly a whole lot worse. It is not an exaggeration to say that she has been my salvation.

The courtship developed and I proposed. After a considerable pause for reflection, Sally agreed. So now, as etiquette then dictated, I had formally to ask Sally's father for his daughter's hand in marriage: this was particularly daunting knowing that he was a headmaster.

The encounter was not as I had anticipated it. I found Mr Taylor relaxing in an armchair wreathed in cigarette smoke and with a large tumbler of sherry by his side. What was more surprising was that he was covered from head to foot in grass cuttings. It transpired that one of his favourite pastimes was mowing the golf course with the gang mower which he drove at great speed creating great clouds of grass cuttings above his head.

I made my request.

"Yes," he said, "that's fine. Now let's go and play some golf."

I explained that I did not play golf.

"Nonsense!" he declared as he led me across the front lawn.

Suddenly he stopped and bellowed, "Caddy."

At this, about fifty little boys in boiler suits emerged from the bushes to offer their services.

Thus it was that my first attempt at hitting a golf ball was witnessed by a large crowd of boys, all expecting heroics.

Sadly, my effort dribbled no more than a few feet along the ground. There was an embarrassed silence, then one little boy, who is now a leading light in the diplomatic service, exclaimed, "Jolly good shot, sir."

I do not remember meeting Mrs Taylor on this first occasion. That was reserved for the next encounter which was dinner at the Swiss Centre in London followed by seats at *Fiddler on the Roof*. I was ill prepared for this as I did not have a suit. Nothing daunted, I borrowed one from a friend. Unfortunately, it was checked and several sizes too small. I am afraid I cut a miserable figure with all the appearance of an unsuccessful spiv.

Sally's mother, on the other hand, was grand, rather in the style of Lady Bracknell. I kept expecting her to say, "'You can hardly imagine that I and Mr Taylor would dream of allowing our daughter – a girl brought up with the utmost care – to marry into a checked suit, and form an alliance with a spiv?'

In the event she said nothing but ignored me the entire evening. *Fiddler on the Roof* was poignant. "If I were a rich man ..." Indeed.

I cannot imagine I passed my first two interviews, but Sally was loyal and determined so the parents had no choice but to persevere. The next date was on the cabin cruiser which was kept on the Norfolk Broads. Decorum dictated that I should sleep in the rear cabin with Mr Taylor whilst Sally slept with her Mum in the fore cabin.

The problem with this was that after several glasses of whisky Mr Taylor was quickly asleep and snoring like a Stentorian. The whole boat reverberated. Then I heard a terrifying cry from the front cabin. It was Sally's mother. "Hit him, David. For God's sake hit him."

This placed me in a dilemma. I rather liked Mr Taylor and did not want to blot my copybook as a prospective son-in-law, but Mrs Taylor had the bearing and presence of one who must be obeyed. I duly swiped the adjacent bunk with my pillow. The snoring stopped momentarily but then resumed with a renewed vigour such that I had not one wink of sleep the entire night.

The wedding was fine. Sally arrived at the altar in tears, which was understandable, but the vicar had a supply of tissues up his sleeve and explained that this sort of thing often happened. I was not wholly convinced.

We had a honeymoon at Sunny Beach in Bulgaria which was all we could afford.

# Chapter 4

# Aged Parents

Dad settled to a reclusive routine when he retired. He would spend most days in his workshop producing incredibly clever carvings and paintings. In the evenings he would switch on the television, turn up the volume high and watch continuously until bedtime. In truth, he only half watched it because he would be reading and researching at the same time, with his board across his knees. This meant that no conversation was possible. Inexplicably, the *Black and White Minstrel Show* was a favourite, and dad had the annoying habit of tapping his pencil supposedly in time with the music. He had no sense of rhythm. I endured long evenings of this, with my Mum sitting opposite sighing and raising her eyes to the sky.

Dad died a slow and painful death from cancer. I regret that we were never reconciled. When I went to visit him in hospital, he commented that it must be bad if I was there. I should have tried to talk with him and to understand him better, but I suppose I was still frightened of him.

Mum lived a lot longer, but her later years were not happy. She was an inveterate worrier and was only ever really at peace when she was sketching and preparing her illuminations.

My eldest sister lived next door to Mum during these years and was saintly in her devoted care.

Sally's Mum was happier in retirement, learning to cook and taking meals on wheels to old folk who were about the same age as herself.

Mr Taylor devoted part of his retirement to trying to turn me into a golfer which was all he had ever really wanted in a son-in-law. This was a hopeless task, but I am not sure that his tactics were right. The club he belonged to for fifty years was so dated it had a separate bar for the women and a separate course for the artisans. The quality of a round was judged not by the number of shots you took but by how long it took you to play the eighteen holes. In one of my earlier rounds, I teed off into the dense rough, as was my custom. As we were searching in vain for the ball, two retired colonels were standing on the tee in their plus fours, grunting and looking distinctly impatient. Richard spotted them and bellowed, "Come on through. I've got a complete rabbit here." And a complete rabbit I remained. Mercifully both my sons proved to be good sportsmen and went a long way to offset the ineptitude of their father.

Sadly Sally's father suffered from dementia in his later years. For a while some wonderful carers looked after him at home, but this became increasingly difficult to sustain. Sometimes we would give the carers a break by sending Richard to a home for a couple of weeks. We would pretend this was a hotel and a holiday, and for the most part he went along with that. However, I remember on one occasion picking him up and asking how it had been. "Fine," he replied, "but it's the only bally hotel I have ever been to that didn't have a bar." He liked his whisky, did Mr Taylor.

Before his memory was totally shot to pieces, we thought it would be good to take Richard to see his brother who was two years younger but who was going the same way. It was a long and tiring journey, but Sally had the bright idea of taking a photograph album of when the two of them were boys. Often sufferers from dementia can remember the more distant past even though they cannot remember what they had for breakfast.

For an hour or so the two brothers sat happily reminiscing. Then suddenly Richard stopped, stared at his brother and declared, "You look awfully like my brother!"

The first home we found was grim – far from cheap but still serving tinned spaghetti hoops for supper. The carers were mainly strident and bossy and did not appear to care much.

The second home was a lot better.

These were sad times but nonetheless punctuated with lighter moments. I once visited Richard only to discover another gentleman in his room. I said I did not want to interrupt and made to leave.

"Not a bit of it," declared the stranger, offering his hand. "The name's Somerset, as in the county. I have just got back from Brussels. Working with the IMF."

"Oh. You are friend of Richard's?"

"Yes. Yes. We go back a long way, don't we Richard?"

At this Richard taps his nose with his finger and gives the stranger a confidential wink.

"We met in New York. Top secret stuff, y'know." Somerset.

Well, what I did know was that Richard had never been to New York in his entire life. Discreet enquiries after the encounter revealed that Mr Somerset was another inmate sharing his fantasy world with Richard.

By the end, Richard had had enough. He stopped eating and died peacefully with his family around him. Richard was a born optimist and one of his favourite phrases on the golf course was, "There are worse places to be." This when your ball had disappeared into the impenetrable rough and was almost certainly lost.

I hope now he finds himself in a state where he can assert again that there are worse places to be. I was very fond of Richard and I shall be forever grateful that he trusted me with two of the things that were most precious to him, his elder daughter and his school.

# Chapter 5

# Teaching

I found myself drifting towards a teaching career for want of anything better to do. This involved a year's study for a Certificate of Education at Cambridge. I found accommodation with Mrs Ivy Boot whilst, remarkably, Sally lodged with Mrs Shoesmith. Before taking up a teaching role she briefly had a job delivering spare parts to garages. There was a quite remarkable surge in demand for these.

The teaching qualification was necessary, but I can't say that I learned much. I remember one lecturer thumping his lectern and declaring that unless one had a clear taxonomy of objectives one would never succeed as a teacher. He was not a firelighter.

I started my teaching career in private secondary schools, known perversely as public schools. If I am honest, I was not much good. An effective teacher needs to be steeped in his/her subject and passionate about it. I was neither.

Surprisingly after three years I was given a job at what was largely regarded as a "top" public school. This was a mistake, both for the school and for me. I suspect I was awarded an interview because my father-in-law knew the headmaster and had sent some boys to the school.

The interview was not what I had expected. It took place one evening in the Headmaster's sitting room where we sat and chatted about this and that over a couple of glasses of wine.

The next day I was surprised and alarmed to learn that I had been given the job. The future Head of my department was not only surprised but horrified. The minimum qualification for an appointment at this school was a good degree from Oxford or Cambridge, preferably with a blue.

And I was indeed out of my depths. Most of the boys had better brains than me and my short exposure to the Oxbridge class was quickly terminated. At least I would be useful for taking the games sessions for the few boys in the school who had no sporting ability.

During my time at the school, it was decided to produce a staff play and *The Magistrate* by Arthur Pinero was chosen. It was a farce – the play, I mean, not the performance. No, the headmaster took the lead role and was most impressive. I was given the part of Cis Faringdon, a rather brainless young man. I probably carried this off quite well.

Married life at this stage was slightly blighted by the fact that we appeared unable to have children. We decided to have a dog instead and bought a pedigree springer spaniel which we named Freda. For some reason, possibly financial, we decided to let her have a litter of puppies and to our astonishment she produced twelve in one go. The vet wanted us to put four of them down, but we hadn't the heart to. Instead, I fed them all from a medicine drip in the garden shed. The night feed was the worst. In their excitement the puppies would scrabble at my pyjama bottoms, causing them to descend. As it was midwinter, this was an uncomfortable experience.

Inevitably, shortly after this, Sally became pregnant and gave birth to our first-born, Jim. One of her friends wrote to congratulate us and asked whether the dog was wondering where the other eleven were! Jim was a handsome baby and one of my colleagues questioned how it was possible that I could have fathered such a good-looking child. It did seem odd.

The other miraculous thing about Jim is that he was remarkably good at sport and I was to spend many a happy hour on the boundary relishing his success and pretending that it all came from me.

I had just one moment of success at the school. I formed a Junior Dramatic Society and produced *Twelfth Night*. The production was good and met with general approval. I still treasure the encouraging notes I received from some my most formidable colleagues.

Not long after this Sally's parents decided to retire, and I was invited to apply for the headmastership of the prep school they had been running for many years. My head of department urged me to apply partly because he wanted to get rid of me, but also (and mainly) because he thought I would be much better suited to this role. In this he was correct.

# Chapter 6

# The Prep School

"Education is not about filling pails: it is about lighting fires."

I was shortlisted with another man who had run a prep school for many years which was proposing to merge with our school. This had its attractions as numbers were well down but amazingly the governors decided to opt for me. I think a large part of the reasoning was that they knew Sally was an absolute gem who had a huge heart for the school and an amazing commitment to it. She was also an outstandingly good teacher.

I was very glad and grateful to be given the chance. I thought I could do it, especially with Sally alongside me, and I was determined to give it my very best shot.

Looking back, it seems surprising to me now that I took on the running of what was then primarily a boarding prep school when I had had such an unhappy experience of boarding myself. At the time I suspect I gave this little consideration, but I like to think now that I wanted to develop a school that was very different from the ones that I had experienced. Quite a lot of the parents were in the Forces or the Foreign Office and sent their children to board out of necessity rather than choice, but whatever the reason for the children being there, I wanted the school to be a happy place and a place that lit fires. I wanted to promote a love of learning and an ethos of service, care and kindness.

It was going to be a challenge. Richard and Pat, as they had now become, had run a very successful and happy school for many years. In many respects they were the ideal couple to run a prep school. For a start they both loved children. In fact, in many respects Richard was still a boy at heart ... and he was always full of enthusiasm and fun.

Many pupils will remember building camps, and the wonderful system Mr T invented for "registering" the camps ... his fiendish obstacle course on Sports day ... the fact that you had to beat him at table tennis or billiards to win the device on your shield. There were games of giants and ogres round the school on dark nights, and *Strictly Come Dancing* in the front hall of a winter evening. And on a winter's day the golf course was transformed into ski slopes and toboggan runs.

He liked to produce the annual play and one old boy recalls Richard showing a trio of puzzled but willing 12-year-olds in rehearsal exactly how one should play the witches' scene from *Macbeth*, complete with a frightening demonstration of his repertoire of banshee wailing and twirling headscarves. I am told that it led to a quite riveting and terrifying performance from the boys!

Sometimes Richard's enthusiasm got the better of him. He was once umpiring a cricket match against the school's arch rivals. The game was in a tense situation with the home side badly needing a breakthrough, when one of the opposition batsmen was struck smartly on his pads. The home team appealed to a boy, and Richard, forgetting that he was the umpire, indeed forgetting himself completely, went up with them all bellowing, "Howzat!" as only he knows how. Realising, however, that he was appealing to himself, he decided to ignore the fact that the boy was plumb lbw, attempting to restore a semblance of objectivity by giving him not out.

Pat complemented him perfectly. She was very well organised – she loved to make lists – and she was very good with detail. She was also a wonderful teacher, and the children loved her reading stories. Gradually it became her habit to down a couple of gin and tonics before undertaking the dormitory rounds. This caused one perceptive little boy to observe that she had exactly the same perfume as his Mum!

However, it is fair to say that towards the end of their time at the school the two of them had rather run out of steam. Numbers were down – a motley collection of 84 boarding boys – and the facilities and fabric of the school were falling behind those of competitors. There was a very real possibility that the school would fail, and this did help to concentrate the mind.

The school building was Victorian and resembled a prison. The cemented walls were covered in algae. For three years I dedicated the holidays to sanding down and sand texting the entire building. This was an unpleasant and precarious task: it involved donning goggles and tying a drying-up cloth round my face and then working off a ladder for the most part. I did have student help and when we needed to reach above the first floor, we erected our own scaffolding. We were not skilled at this, and I shudder now to consider the risks we took.

On one occasion I was sanding away when I heard a loud "OI!" at the bottom of the scaffold. I duly descended. The man at the bottom addressed me in quite a surly manner and wanted to know whether he could speak with the headmaster. When I removed the goggles and drying-up cloth and declared that "I am he" he seemed somewhat taken aback. Remarkably he decided to send his son to the school. I say remarkably because it turns out he was a fireman and would have known what ridiculous risks I was taking with ladders and scaffold.

The staff were pleasant and wonderfully tolerant when faced with this upstart leader, appointed as a result of outrageous nepotism. Many had shown wonderful loyalty to my in-laws and the school.

Mrs S was one such. She arrived at the school at an age when many would be, and indeed are, considering retirement, and she served the school selflessly for over forty years. She was the queen of the front office which was the hub of the school. She kept all the books by hand, answered the telephone, acted as receptionist and headmaster's secretary, issued ping pong balls to the children and John Player cigarettes to the staff and maintained a fine tradition of thriftiness: "Books!" I remember her exclaiming, "What do you want books for?" She knew the truth of the saying, "Look after the penny and the pound will look after itself."

The front office boasted an open fire in the early days, and it was the responsibility of Mr de L to lay and light the fire each morning. Mr de L suffered from wind and a dark sense of humour. From time to time, he would provide a commentary on the way things were going which was not altogether heartening for the new headmaster. "Chaos with a capital K," he would pronounce.

Being the least likely to complain, my office accommodation regularly changed to accommodate others. However, it never really seemed to matter where they put me because I invariably spent most of my time in the front office in the armchair by the fire. This was partly because I enjoyed the company, but also because it was an endless source of entertainment. There were other habitués: the history teacher spent a lot of time in there on the telephone to his impresarios discussing the relative merits of Shostakovich and Schoenberg for his next concert, with a pencil stuck in one ear to blot out unwanted noises; the photocopy repair man was almost always there, spraying something which smelt suspiciously like chloroform into the machine; the computer guru was often there to rescue one of the ladies from a scroll lock and there were usually a couple of children reporting some disaster in the grounds. Indeed, one boy brought in a live grenade which he had found in the bushes, left over, one imagines, from the RAF occupation of the school during the war. Careless.

The office boasted an alcove. It was curtained so that visitors could not see the mess and muddle on the shelves behind. I think I can safely admit now that it was my custom when I saw a particularly difficult parent approaching the office, to hide behind the curtain. This was difficult for the receptionist who had to declare that the headmaster was not available even when she could see his feet sticking out from under the curtain.

Charlie was another stalwart. For 35 years he looked after the estate of 50 acres, sports fields and all, with only a little help from Mr Taylor with the mowing of the golf course. He was born and bred a Sussex man: he called potatoes "Tayters", was patient enough to shoot moles and could tell what weather was coming from the state of the shrubs.

Eric was the kitchen porter. He was one of the chattiest people I have ever met, but unfortunately, he had a speech impediment, so it was difficult to understand what he was saying. He had a wonderful sense of humour and a raucous laugh to give it expression. His domain was the pantry which was sited alongside the dining room where each morning we held the school assembly. This meant that just as we were launching into the Lord's Prayer – "our Father, who art in Heaven" – gales of unbridled laughter would reverberate through the hatch. On one occasion Eric laughed so energetically that he collapsed and had to be tended by the school doctor. As we filed out of the dining room, one little boy politely enquired of me, "Who's that man who has just died down the passage?" Mercifully Eric had not died.

Generally, Eric was held in much affection by the children. My nephew, who was a boarder at the school, was so fond of him that he insisted his family address him as Eric at home for one entire summer holiday.

Pleasant as the teaching staff undoubtedly were, there was possibly a little lack of dynamism. I sought to address this with my first appointment which was made before the start of my first term. It was a new French teacher (Mr M) who had the distinction of boasting a splendid Lotus Elan and equally splendid French wife. The couple were recently married and had been given a precious heirloom by the French family – a large double bed.

Unfortunately, this would not go up the staircase of the little school cottage in which the couple were to be housed. Mr M was insistent, so the school carpenter dutifully removed the staircase. The bed was still too big.

It was then that Mr M suggested that we took out two of the upstairs windows and part of the wall to accommodate the siting of the bed. This seemed a little drastic, but Mr M announced that he would not start his job unless the bed was accommodated. I could see why the bed was important to him, but I felt this was going too far.

Eventually a compromise was reached, and the couple agreed to have their bedroom downstairs and their sitting room upstairs.

You will appreciate that Mr M was a determined man and he proved very good at ensuring that the children learned their French vocabulary each week. In the event he did not last long but went on to be a tax inspector, a job for which he was eminently well qualified.

The senior master was a Mr DB who taught Latin. He was a kindly man but not very good at keeping order. One of the school inspectors who visited the school early on told me that he sat at the back of Mr DB's class, only to hear a boy in front of him say to his neighbour, "Oh do shut up. The inspector can't hear a word DB is saying."

Mrs DB was at the other end of the spectrum. She ruled Form 2 with a rod of iron and was possibly the most frightening woman I have ever met.

There was a housemaster who had been appointed on the grounds that he had been a Major in the army, when in fact he had been a Sergeant Major. You could tell the difference.

So, there were staff changes. At one point I invited Mr Taylor back to teach geography. This was a mistake. He developed the habit of falling asleep in staff meetings and snoring loudly. Whilst accepting that the proceedings were dull, I did find this disconcerting.

The fabric of the classrooms and dormitories was generally as bad as that of the outside of the house. For some reason we entrusted a boy to show prospective parents round the boarding house, and sometimes the parents reported back to us. On one occasion the little boy had taken his visitors to Eagles dormitory. This was one that I usually omitted from my tours because, as its name suggests, it was found up several flights of stairs. It was also in quite the worst state of any dormitory in the school – uneven floorboards designed to give the boys splinters, iron beds, draughty windows and peeling paint. The parents were surprised, then, when the little boy swung open the door and pronounced that this was the best dormitory in the school. When the parents looked puzzled and unconvinced, he added confidentially, "It's the furthest from matron."

Gradually we smartened up the school (carpeted classrooms). and built the numbers.

Quite early on we decided to take girls which proved to be a good decision. The term after the first girls arrived, I was taking an English class and challenging the children to complete pairings. You know the sort of thing, "Trouble and ..."; "Cloak and ..."; "Gin and ...". When I presented them with "Kith and ..." one little boy rejected the standard "Kith and kin" and came with a much better pairing, "Kith and cuddle."

Mind you, having the girls and boys boarding accommodation within the same building did cause some problems on occasions. At one point there was a spate of girls "raiding" boys' dormitories and vice versa. Now the term "raiding" was coined by the children, and I am not quite sure what was involved but I have to hope it was largely innocent.

Nonetheless, Sally decided she would put a stop to it. Her strategy was to sleep overnight in a box room that was situated in between the girls' and boys' quarters. As she heard the patter of tiny feet she would leap out and catch them all red-handed. What she did not know was that one of the boys had the habit of using the box room as somewhere to read when he was unable to sleep.

That night he padded to the room, quietly opened the door and switched on the light. Imagine his horror when he discovered the headmaster's wife fast asleep on the sofa. He switched off the light, shut the door and beat a hasty retreat.

We later learned that the boy wrote in his letter home at the weekend, "Dear Mum and Dad, I am very sorry to have to tell you that the Chaplin marriage is in big trouble."

We had some amazingly patient and dedicated matrons. Unfortunately, one had a little Jack Russell which she used to keep in her room. As I was conducting my prospective parent tour the wretched dog would bark ferociously and throw itself at the door. I would smile weakly and explain that this was matron's wee dog, but in truth I would have gladly had the animal shot.

We had another matron from South Africa whose pronunciation of the casual term for wellington boots sounded awfully like "willies". She was forever reminding the children to put their willies away, an instruction that confused the girls.

The first ten years at the school were busy but happy as we saw the school gradually moving in the right direction. We were also blessed with the gift of two more lovely children, a girl and a boy, and they were able to benefit from going to the school on their doorstep.

Inevitably there were low moments and crises. One such was when two of the boys decided to run away, taking their pet rabbit with them on a lead. This happened one Saturday afternoon and I am bound to admit that it was only at tea-time that we realised they were missing.

Initially, we ran round the perimeter of the grounds calling their names and checking all likely hiding places.

As time wore on, I had no option but to call the parents. One set lived overseas, so this was especially difficult, and another lived just a few miles from the school. We agreed that they should stay put in case the boys turned up there.

As dusk began to fall, I felt it necessary to call the police. Imagine the drama as two cars with flashing lights parked outside the front door of the school.

It was then decided to call upon a heat-seeking helicopter. It circled the school for a while and then landed in a field nearby. I had the dreadful notion that they had discovered the boys' bodies, but mercifully no.

Eventually the parents living nearby could bear the tension no longer and decided to drive up to the school. On their way they found the boys walking along the road, picked them up (and the rabbit) and brought them back to our huge relief.

At this point the mother of the boy who lived nearby suggested to her son that he apologise for all the trouble he had caused and hurry off to bed.

The policeman could not believe his ears. "What!" he cried. "Your son is so unhappy at school that he has run away, and you are still not taking him home."

"No," replied my heroic Mum, perfectly calmly. "My son is very happy at this school. His running away was just an adventure that went badly wrong."

Needless to say, I thought that the mother was right, and I was immensely grateful for her trust and support at this critical time.

We enjoyed wonderful moments to offset the difficult ones.

At one point we had a Jack Russell (a boy, not the matron's dog) in the school, two Barkers and a Yap (from Hong Kong). Who should come to look round the school but Mr and Mrs Woof! When I explained that they simply must send their son to the school to complete the canine theme they were not amused and sent the boy to our arch-rivals down the road. So forever we were deprived of the opportunity of ending our roll call with a Woof and a Yap!

I have always enjoyed names. My headmaster at secondary school was called Alan Barker. He was married to Lady Trumpington. They both made a lot of noise.

My elder son spent a year teaching at a school in Zimbabwe. His headmaster there was English and had a double-barrelled name: he was called Mr Shaw-Twilley.

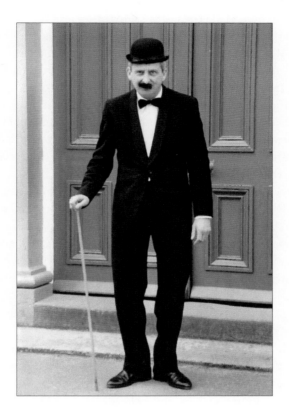

I continued to enjoy dressing up. From time to time, we would set aside a day for charity when the children and staff were encouraged to come to school as a chosen character. It seemed logical that I should appear as Charlie Chaplin.

A little unwisely I remained in costume to show some prospective parents round the school but mercifully on this occasion the parents did have a sense of humour and duly enrolled their children.

One night we had a break-in. It was bold burglars who broke into a school with a hundred children sleeping upstairs. They could have had no idea what potential chaos they might have unleashed. In truth I think they were drunk. It seems they settled in the kitchen, made themselves cups of tea and then proceeded to raid the stores. They made off with a peculiar horde – catering packs of Danish bacon, cornflakes, tins of jam and a microwave oven – all packed into the children's sports bags, the contents of which they threw all over the changing room floor.

In the morning Sally discovered the mayhem in the changing rooms and, unaware of what had actually happened, marched into breakfast and commanded the children not to eat another mouthful until they had been to clear up the mess. Understandably they were utterly bewildered.

Days later we were putting the final touches to our insurance claim when the police rang to say they had recovered our lost property and would I travel to Shoreham-by- Sea to reclaim it. This was not altogether good news. It was quite a trip, and I had to spend a long afternoon signing pieces of paper affirming that this catering pack of cornflakes was the one purloined from the school. The whole business took the best part of two hours. Halfway through the procedure the constable in charge of the operation nudged me and observed, "Not much like *The Bill*, is it?"

In 1987 the hurricane struck. It took us a while to appreciate the gravity of the situation. Sally was the first to look out of the window to see that the bike sheds had blown over the wall and landed in our garden. She observed that there had been a rather violent storm: knowing that she was given to hyperbole, I said, "Yes, dear," rolled over and went back to sleep. Moments later the housemaster was banging on the front door. "I think you need to come to the school."

What we discovered was apocalyptic. Hundreds of trees had been uprooted, crushing a couple of classrooms and destroying the tennis courts. In the main school the glass roof lights were all smashed, and the children were confined to their dormitories. However, they were all remarkably calm and sensible and gradually we began to establish a way forward. One challenge was that we were without any electricity and this persisted for very nearly three weeks. We did not have the option of sending all the children home as we had over 100 boarders, many of them from families overseas.

The night after the storm I sat down with the children for a candlelit supper. The little boy next to me tugged my arm and asked, with a conspiratorial air, "Do you think there'll be another one tonight sir?"

The job of clearing up was massive and several cowboys offered their services. "We can clear this lot for you, sir. No problem." "Oh, good. And how much would that be?" "Well now, Guv'nor. We're in big demand. Shall we say £50,000?"

I was just resigning myself to tearing up the development plan when one of the parents rang, He was the colonel to a regiment of Gurkha soldiers. "Would you like a couple of my men to come and clear the trees?" They arrived with their chain saws and had the place clear in a couple of weeks.

The army was good to us on other occasions. A former pupil, who was flying Sea King helicopters rang me up and asked whether I would like him to land his helicopter at the school. I jumped at the opportunity. I had the entire school lined up overlooking the junior football pitch and at exactly the appointed hour the helicopter flew low over the school, performed a couple of circuits and landed. The pilot climbed out mopping his brow and looking rather distressed. "Is everything OK?" I enquired.

"Yes," he replied, "but when I was a pupil at the school, I thought this pitch was quite big!"

I suppose I ought to confess that I used this occasion to play an unkind trick. I told the cook, who was a lovely lady called Jean, that Prince Charles and Princess Diana were flying in to look round the school for their boys – the timing was about right. "Oh Lord," she exclaimed as she straightened her apron and patted her hair, "and I've only got sausages for lunch."

The army also provided us with a rope bridge for fourth year camp.

Fourth year camp requires explanation. Originally the school had boasted its own cub and scout packs, and when these were abandoned, the tradition was retained of taking all the ten-year-olds camping for a long weekend. This was a demanding and perilous exercise which became increasingly difficult to staff and, in the end, the only person who could be persuaded to run it was the headmaster which he did for fifteen long years.

The children were all allocated to groups named after Roman tribes – Amazones, Atrebates, Brigantes and the like. We were hosted at a former pupil's farm in Kent and the site was perfect, grassy woodland with river for fishing running by. Each tribe would set up its camp independently, dig its own loo pit and cook its own food over an open fire,

Furthermore, it became a custom to string a rope bridge (courtesy of the army) across the river which each child was dared to wobble across.

Can you imagine what health and safety would have to say about all this?

There is no way a school could contemplate such an exercise now, and yet many of the pupils will remember fourth year camp as a highlight of their time at the school.

Knowing from my own experience how daunting it can be for some people to speak in public, we were glad to be able introduce the English Speaking Board to the school. This required all the children to give a talk each year on a subject about which they were passionate. They also had to recite a poem and read from a novel of their choice. Apart from encouraging a love of reading, this also developed the children's confidence in public speaking. The talks had to be carefully prepared and the children were encouraged to use props and visual aids. They then spoke to an audience of fifty or so and fielded questions at the end. It was amazing how even quite timid children grew to be good at doing this, and how well it went on to serve them in later life.

I still remember many of the talks. One girl spoke about her grandfather who had been a Japanese prisoner of war. Her visual aid was his belt. She showed us the buckle it was on when he was captured and the buckle when he was released. It was very powerful.

She also told us that he had received a tin of tomatoes in one of the rare food parcels that reached him. He carefully picked out and planted the seeds and this helped him to survive.

Another boy spoke about his dinky toys. On the face of it this was not a promising subject, but in the event it was fascinating. He had an amazing collection including one car which appeared to flash its headlights when you held it up to a window.

Gradually we began to develop the facilities at the school and each time we opened a new building we used the opportunity to invite a guest who would be inspirational for the children.

Our first new building housed science laboratories and David Bellamy came along. You may remember this bearded naturalist who often appeared on television, usually in a ditch. He was the very epitome of a good teacher – full of enthusiasm and very knowledgeable. He spent the entire day with us and seemed reluctant to go home at the end of it all. Here was a man who could light a fire.

Next was a new pre-preparatory school and this time Neil Buchanan did the honours. He organised a special Art Attack for the children which they greatly enjoyed.

For some reason we did not have a guest at the opening of the new theatre but perhaps that was because we produced two plays in one week – *Midsummer Night's Dream* for the older children and *The Wizard of Oz* for the youngsters.

The theatre was a great addition to the facilities. The previous arrangements had left a lot to be desired: the theatre, such as it was, had been housed at the end of the indoor swimming pool. Remarkably the pool had been built by the school's own builder who was called appropriately Harry Wash. It was a considerable achievement, but it did have its shortcomings: the insulation was poor and the system for heating the air above the pool inadequate, so it was always steamed up and dripping.

The sound and lighting equipment in the theatre at the end were not extensive but even in their simplicity, they objected to the steamy atmosphere and regularly fused. As a consequence, several scenes of the school plays were conducted in complete darkness, and the sound effects for the whole of *The Thwarting of Baron Bolligrew* were provided by the deputy headmaster from behind the scenery.

The proximity to the swimming pool did, however, prove an advantage on one occasion. Unwisely I took on the part of Fagin in *Oliver.*" When I came out with the line, "I'm a real miser, you know," the audience broke into spontaneous applause. I think the fees had just gone up.

Then at the end of the first half whilst singing "I'm reviewing the situation" I managed to swallow a bit of my beard. I think I might well have choked to death had I not been able to douse my head in the adjacent swimming pool during the interval,

In the new theatre we produced three or four plays each year, usually ending with a musical. On one occasion we chose *Salad Days* and one of the boys announced during a rehearsal that his godfather was Julian Slade and he was coming to see the show. I am afraid I thought he was pulling my leg, so I was a little taken aback when Mr Slade did turn up for the final performance. I sat a few seats away from him and after a few minutes he turned to his neighbour and whispered, "This is really quite good." I took that as a huge compliment.

We generally produced at least one nativity play at Christmas. One year I had rashly appointed an extremely tiresome boy as Joseph in the hope that the glory of the part might prompt him to behave. The stratagem failed and Joseph spent most of the rehearsals pinching the angels or harassing the sheep. In the end I had had enough and decided to demote him from Joseph to the innkeeper who had only two words to say.

Come the night of the performance the parents arrived in eager anticipation of seeing their young ones perform and the headmaster/producer looked on benevolently. All went well until Mary and Joseph arrived at the inn and knocked on the door.

"Do you have any rooms?" inquires Joseph. "My wife is about to give birth."

The innkeeper grins broadly and replies, "Yes. Plenty."

I heard once that a teacher "up north" was telling the nativity story with the problem at the inn to her class when one little boy put his hand up and said, "Please Miss, I blame Joseph."

"Why is that?" asks the teacher.

"Well, Miss, he should have booooked."

The theatre was a wonderful venue for music as well as plays. There had not been a strong tradition of music-making in the school when we arrived. In one of the early concerts a little boy called Bruce played *The Bluebells of Scotland* on his violin. It was so excruciating I can still remember it as if it happened yesterday. It might have been Bruce who came out of his violin examination, Grade 1, and announced that he thought the examiner must be religious. When asked why he explained that he kept putting his head in his hands and crying, "Oh God!"

Standards gradually improved so that by the time the theatre was built there was every type of ensemble group, orchestra and choir to perform in it. Not only was it wonderful for the school musicians, but the history teacher set up an annual series of subscription concerts which have flourished for over 30 years. Local people are delighted to be able hear top class musicians playing without having to make the trek to London.

Most of the repertoire is classical and we have enjoyed visits from some of the top string quartets, pianists and other ensembles.

Occasionally, something a little lighter was included. One year Humphrey Lyttelton and his jazz band played. They were hugely entertaining, but the morning after I was surprised to be woken at the crack of dawn by a little boy announcing that the art room was on fire.

I rushed to the scene and was there just in time as the room was indeed full of smoke and about to burst into flames. It transpired that the band had used the room as a green room and the double bass player had left his cigar in a plant pot. I tried to persuade Humphrey that this was reason enough to return and give us a concert for free, but he was not convinced.

We had a fundraising campaign to buy a grand piano for the use of the school and the concert performers. To this end we invited Peter Skellern to come to sing for us. He arrived in the afternoon to rehearse. As he did so, the history teacher rushed into the office with a white coat which he ordered me to put on. When questioned he explained that he had agreed to provide a sound engineer for the performer but had forgotten to do so. As I produced a lot of the plays, he decided I was the next best thing.

I duly went down to the theatre and into the lighting and sound room. Peter Skellern was on stage rehearsing. When he saw that I was in situ, he started bellowing up instructions. "More flutter on channel three." "Less verb on channel five."

I hadn't a clue what he was talking about and twiddled a few knobs in hope. Eventually he stopped playing, marched to the back of the theatre, flung open the door of the lighting room and declared, "You're not a sound engineer, are you?"

"No," I replied, "I am the headmaster."

I don't think he saw the funny side, but he did perform a wonderful concert, including his one hit, "*You're a Lady*" and a delicious rendering of *The Way you Look Tonight*. I still occasionally sing the latter to Sally before we go off to sleep. "Lovely, never ever change ..." This is intended to be romantic and winning.

Imagine my disappointment when in return Sally sings for me, *Here Comes Muffin, Muffin the Mule*.

I do believe that our commitment to the performing arts lit fires and contributed a lot to the success of the school. Parents and children loved the concerts and plays, and children gained great confidence from performing. It is no surprise that quite a number of pupils have gone on to musical or theatrical careers: we boast three members of the band Keane, one boy is a director at the Globe Theatre, one of our girls sang the lead in *The Phantom of the Opera* for several years and another girl is a successful opera singer.

Next it was sports hall and one of the parents persuaded the golfer, Peter Alliss, to spend the day with us. He was wonderful, so generous with his time and such fun. To give the lunch a little more class, my daughter agreed to act as a waitress, the main task being to recharge Peter's wine glass. She was amazed at how often this was required, but we all agreed that the only effect of him drinking prodigiously was to make him still more kindly and congenial.

Our last project was a millennium Learning Centre. This time John Simpson officiated. I thought he would be interesting for the parents, but I was not so sure he would engage with the children. In this I was entirely wrong. He invited them to ask questions and because of their ESB training they asked some good ones. JS had a wonderful way of answering these with a series of stories and anecdotes. And has he some good stories to tell! What was your most embarrassing moment? Ah, that was when his trousers split in the presence of the Queen. And the most frightening. Tiananmen Square, of course.

Similarly, I tried to find good speakers for prize-giving. Politicians were to be avoided at all costs.

I had two outstanding successes. Sir Tim Smit, of Eden Project fame, was a former pupil of the school. He arrived in t shirt and jeans and began by declaring that the audience probably didn't want to listen to a boring old fart like him. He was far from boring. He spoke with passion about our need to care for the planet and I feel sure that there are pupils whose lives have been informed by his vision.

The cosmonaut, Helen Sharman, was similarly inspirational. She told us that she had been working for Mars, the confectionery people: the press loved this given what she went on to do. She was driving home one day listening to the radio and it was announced that the Russians were looking for a cosmonaut for their next space mission. Helen applied along with 30,000 other people. In the end she was chosen, trained and proved to be the first woman in space. What a fabulous message for a prize-giving! Who knows what you can achieve if you aim high?

Helen's talk was superb, describing the humbling feeling as she sat and watched the Earth diminish to the size of a tennis ball. She also talked about the strangeness of being weightless.

Good questions at the end. One eight-year-old boy wanted to know how she went to the loo!

Not all the visits were successful. We had a man who came with a collection of animals – a hawk and an owl amongst them. The speaker invited lots of volunteers to help and I tried to make myself invisible because I could see what was coming. Sure enough. He came to his last animal. "Now," he declared, "we need one more volunteer. Ah! What about the headmaster?"

Up I went on stage and to my horror a large snake was wrapped around my neck. Worse was to follow. I don't suppose snakes have tails, but the end that was opposite the head found its way down my back and between my legs. I prayed that it wasn't a boa constrictor. The audience seemed to be enjoying all this. Quite a few of the mothers came to the front and photographed me in my undignified dilemma.

As the years went by, we were inspected more regularly and had to make a greater effort to conform. One of our best teachers was undoubtedly the history teacher, Mr W (not Wildermoth – long since deceased): I make this judgement partly on the basis of the number of children who left the school with a love of the subject and a desire to research it further. However, Mr W was not conventional. He often referred to the children as vermin – not unreasonable – and had an extreme dislike of children who started to pack their things away before the bell had sounded. To counter this, he had what he called his "tin dance" which involved seizing the metal instrument case from the offending child and dancing round the room scattering its contents.

On the morning of one inspection, I sat down to lunch next to a boy who nudged me and declared, "Mr W was completely different this morning."

At one point we were subjected to a boarding inspection. A wily old gentleman led the team and, in the evening, he toured the dormitories with Sally and myself in tow. Towards the end he approached Elephants dormitory and headed for the one boy we would have preferred him to avoid. The boy was a lovely chap called Albert, but he was not renowned for his tact and discretion. The inspector sat on Albert's bed and made casual conversation for a while. Then, when Albert's defences were down, he popped in his leading question.

"Tell me, Albert, do you ever have fire practices?"

Imagine our relief when Albert answered with a cheery, "Yes. We had one last night." Then he added, "It was chaos."

The school was tolerably successful, but we were never likely to allow this to go to our heads as long as there were children around. I remember watching an under -10 football match one afternoon. I was standing behind the goal and I don't think our goalkeeper was aware that I was there. Anyway, he was having trouble getting his kicks away – sometimes he missed the ball completely. Eventually he says to his friend who is the full back, "You take the next kick and pretend the ball's Mr Chaplin's head."

I am bound to record that the ball sailed down the pitch and very nearly scored a goal at the other end.

I suspect that we stayed at the school for too long. Towards the end of my time there I received a letter from one of the parents that began, "Dead headmaster." I wasn't sure whether this was a typing error, a veiled threat or merely a passing observation, but it seemed like the right moment to be moving on.

The school governors had reached the same conclusion and they offered me early retirement with a remarkably generous pension.

When I left the school a lot of the pupils wrote in a book, a book that I shall always treasure. I realise that just as inscriptions on gravestones are almost always positive and generous, so pupils were unlikely to air their grievances in a book that is saying a fond farewell. That said, all of them declared that they had been happy at the school and a lot referred to the camp and to plays as being highlights. One boy wrote as follows:

"I will always remember the unique kindness and happiness you created at the school. I feel you have helped me to achieve my best in all areas."

Now I am not foolish enough to believe that the school I ran was without fault: it had many shortcomings and weaknesses, and I made a lot of mistakes. However, if that boy caught the essence of the school, then I am very glad and grateful.

# Chapter 7

# New Zealand

Leaving the school was in many ways a sad and difficult experience but this was largely offset by the prospect of living in our own house and garden for the first time in our married life. We also planned a visit to New Zealand.

Apart from anything else we thought this would give our successors the space to establish themselves at the school without the spectre of the Chaplins haunting the place. We also knew that New Zealand was a stunningly beautiful country and would afford us the opportunity to visit some of the wonderful Kiwi Gap students who had supported us so brilliantly in the course our twenty-five years at the school.

The plan was to hire a camper van for a few months: this was undoubtedly the riskiest element of the operation.

Sally is not the easiest of passengers when her husband is driving. She has a number of ways of indicating her anxiety or displeasure. Waving her hand in front of her suggests that you are either too near the edge of the road or too near the middle. Tapping the gear lever indicates that you are in the wrong gear. Clutching the side of the seat and gasping suggests that she feels you are going too fast, and placing her feet on the dashboard indicates that she feels you are about to run into the back of the lorry that has just braked 500 yards ahead.

The pressure of her nervousness was relieved somewhat by the fact that there seemed to be precious few cars on the roads in New Zealand. However, the journey was not without incident. The company that hired us the van instructed that every day it was necessary to check the tyre pressures, the oil and water levels and the wastewater sump.

I am afraid I had a somewhat cavalier approach to these instructions. This was not shared by Sally. After a week of carefree motoring, she announced that she would not travel any further until all the checks were carried out.

In a fit of unreasonable pique, I swerved into the next garage and set about the job. The checks complete, I slammed the bonnet shut, climbed into the driver's seat and we resumed the journey.

The next few minutes were passed in silence. Then Sally looked across at me and wanted to know why I was not wearing my driving glasses.

There was a further pregnant pause. I then confessed, a little sheepishly, that I rather thought I had left the spectacles in the engine. In the engine!!!"

Miraculously they were recovered undamaged.

New Zealand did not disappoint. The variety and splendour of the scenery were truly spectacular and the people wonderfully warm and welcoming.

However, it was the visits to our former Kiwi students and their families that were particularly special,

One such was to Tahora Farm in the remote Urewera National Park north of Gisborne.

In Māori, Tahora means "a plentiful clearing in the bush", and this farm was appropriately named. It had been acquired some twenty years previously in a scheme in which the then government cleared native bush and allowed people to bid for the land on a lottery basis. Bidders were ruthlessly scrutinised and those who were successful had to work under very tight supervision, but for those with the necessary determination and acumen, there was the prospect of developing and owning sizeable plots of land under very advantageous circumstances.

Our hosts were N and W and their three sons, one of whom had been a wonderful gapper at our school.

When they arrived at the place N told us it was overgrown and derelict and her inclination was to turn heel with her young family. Instead, she and W "set to". Together they have transformed the land and built up a fine flock of Romney sheep and an equally fine herd of Hereford cattle. Furthermore, their house is surrounded by the most beautiful garden.

They rightly had immense pride in all that they have achieved, and they devoted three entire days to sharing it all with us. What a privilege.

Up in the woods, they have restored an ancient privy which is no more than a "long drop." On the inside of the door are printed the words of an appropriate song: "He sat alone in the still of the night, with thoughts that were far away. He took a pen and started to write, just what his heart had to say. Wait for me, Sally, by the moonlit garden gate."

Another farm visit was to P and R in Waimati. As ever, we were warmly welcomed and P invited us to watch the shearing that was taking place. The shearers hang from pulleys to save their backs, and this is clearly a very skilled and demanding job. Imagine my alarm then, when Peter stopped halfway through a shearing and invited me to finish it off. There was a danger that I would do this in more senses than one.

I am told that that the art of sheep shearing lies not so much in how you handle the blade, but rather more in how you control the sheep. Its head must be positioned between your legs and gripped firmly but not too tightly by your knees.

Miraculously the fleece came away at the end of it all, but I fancy my sheep left the barn a little woollier than its friends.

After all this P's father, B, invited us to visit his nearby farm for a few minutes. B was one of the old school, seemingly hewn out of rock. He had reared sheep for most of his life and had huge fore-arms and massive hands. However, they were surprisingly soft, however, from years of contact with the lanolin in the wool, and he played the piano with remarkable touch and sensitivity.

My goodness, he was tough though. Having earned and saved money as a travelling sheep-shearer, he bought his farm and he and his wife devoted their entire working lives to making a success of it. The only holiday they had ever taken was their three-day honeymoon. B declared that he hated the "bloody sheep" but I am not sure that the evidence bore this out.

He had had some setbacks recently. Two years previously he had been baling straw in one of his fields when he inadvertently failed to engage the tractor handbrake correctly. The tractor rolled down the hill and the steel prong of the bale fork-lifter pierced his leg and pinioned him to a large bale of straw. This happened in the late afternoon, so he was unable to summon help. For seventeen hours and right through the night he was pinned to the bale, his leg smashed and only his dog for warmth, comfort and company. He said it didn't hurt much!

In the morning he was discovered by a passer-by. The steel blade was sawn off the baler and B was flown by helicopter to the nearest hospital with the prong still through his leg. Advised that it would be better not to have a general anaesthetic, B remained conscious whilst they removed the prong and rebuilt his shattered leg. Then he wanted to walk back to the ward!

Later he did lose consciousness, along with six pints of blood, but he was still back home after ten days. A fiercely proud and independent man, he would be beholden to no-one.

One sensed that B could deal with any amount of physical adversity, but what had knocked him for six was the loss of his beloved wife to cancer. He clearly missed her dreadfully and his house was a terrible mess and muddle. Still, he insisted that we stay for supper and he set about making a pie while Sally tried to sort out the kitchen and ward off the cats and the flies.

Then B wondered whether we like mushrooms. We did. So we were bundled into the lambing cart behind the quad bike and we careered off round the farm screeching to a halt whenever a mushroom was spotted.

It was something of a white-knuckle ride, and I noticed, with some annoyance, that not once did Sally produce a hand signal or a cry of alarm.

After the pie, which turned out to be delicious, we retired to the camper van which was parked in the paddock. In the morning we were woken by the aptly named bell birds and bade our farewells. B urged us to revisit, but we had the feeling that we would not see him again, nor, indeed, anyone quite like him.

During our trip the natural world was a constant source of delight. At one point we took a trip across the Picton Sounds to Motuara Island. This was a natural bird sanctuary by virtue of the fact that all mammalian predators had been eliminated.

Peter was our driver and guide, and although a typically tall and chunky Kiwi, he was remarkably gentle, perhaps even a shade precious. "Hello! My name's Peter, and I'm your dwiver," was his opening gambit. "Are you all comfy?"

The Sounds are magnificent. Like a fjord, a sound is a valley that has been filled with sea water. However, a sound is usually formed by the flooding of a river valley, not a glacial valley. This means that the topography is usually less narrow and more gently sloping than a fjord, but it is no less spectacular. Everywhere you look there are three "layers": the pale blue, cloudless sky; then the bush or pine-covered mountains, almost strokable, and a wonderful variety of greens as the light catches them differently; and finally, the vast expanse of turquoise blue water, ruffled silver and white by the sun and the wind.

Soon we were ticking off seabirds with excitement – you can tell we are both teachers! We spotted the alarmingly named King Shag and were told that they are only found in these waters and in dwindling numbers. You'd think they would be good at reproducing.

It was low tide when we arrive at the island, so we had to clamber up some precarious rocks. Our guide told us that there were some rare birds including the saddleback. These had not been seen on the mainland for many years, but 28 birds had been introduced some years previously. Initially they had flourished, and numbers rose to one hundred, but for no obvious reason numbers had recently diminished alarmingly. David, in his usual Eeyore fashion, concluded that there was no chance of seeing them at all.

He was wrong! Towards the end of our walk, we saw a pair of saddlebacks bathing in a pool of water only a few feet away from us. Then, after seeing the beautiful bellbird and hearing its exquisite song, we had sight of the South Island robin searching for insects. I am not known as a twitcher but I defy anyone not to be excited by these amazing birds.

The "Penguin Tour" at Omara was no less exciting. It was quite a long wait but eventually what appeared to be a collection of seaweed on the shoreline struggled to its feet and began to waddle up the beach. There was a careful preening process to be undertaken so the birds were in no hurry, and we were able to admire these yellow-eyed penguins at leisure. We loved their sparkling white bibs, perfect tailcoats and pink webbed feet.

Finally, we visited the only mainland colony of the royal albatross in the world. There we learned that the birds only ever land to find a partner and to breed; they live upwards of forty years, are monogamous and always return to their original colony. Their wingspan is three metres, and they fly on average 500 km per day at an average speed of 50 kph.

None of this matches the experience of seeing these fine birds. Their flight was incredibly graceful, and watching them preening their young, or stretching their necks to exchange joyful sky-calls, was truly memorable. We also saw some adult birds returning to breed after five years at sea. They glided in on the wind but when they landed, they all promptly fell over! Not surprisingly, they had forgotten how to walk.

We loved walking along the beaches spotting spoonbills and stilts. At Sandy Point we had to hurry across some mud flats to beat the tide, and seeing Sally slithering and sliding encouraged me to offer a new entry for Geoff Moon's Book of New Zealand Birds.

"The greater Black-trousered Flounder is a migrant from UK and can occasionally be spotted on the mud flats close to Invercargill. The bird is flightless but is inclined to flap its wings when it is anxious. It moves in an ungainly fashion, often with a shrill cry of "Ivelostashoo! Ivelostashoo!" The male bird has a larger beak and is inclined to loiter unhelpfully in the sand dunes."

Did we go bungee jumping or paragliding? No.

But David was very keen to go white-water rafting. Eventually he managed to persuade Sally to agree, and we went to book the trip at the office in Queenstown. Unfortunately, as we queued, there was a large American recalling his experiences from the day before when his wife fell overboard. "She was a little bruised and shaken," he declared cheerfully, "but I guess if you go overboard you've just got to hang on in and hope that sooner or later your head will come up."

Sally felt unable to accept this philosophical position and our participation in the trip was ruled out.

However, we did have another try at Greymouth. Here Bruce was in charge, and Sally seemed to find him rather attractive and reassuring even though he could not promise her that the boat would not turn over.

In the event the water was not very rapid and Sally seemed to enjoy herself: she even had a go at steering whilst Bruce held her hand.

It was, without doubt, the holiday of a lifetime, but as I undertook my last hill climb, I found myself unusually breathless and I had a nasty feeling that I wasn't very well.

# Chapter 8

# Hospital

I had been fortunate to have faced little or no illness during my entire working life, but as soon as I stopped – indeed, perhaps because I stopped – things took a turn for the worse and I was admitted to hospital with a suspected heart condition. Like all men with a tendency for hypochondria, I did wonder whether this was the beginning of the end of it all, which would have been disappointing. Mercifully, I was wrong.

Until then I had only been in hospital once in my entire life. This was at the age of six when I was admitted to the Jenny Lind in Norwich to have my tonsils out. I do not recall this as an unpleasant experience. The nurse gave me sixpence for singing nicely before the operation, and when I got home, I was given a hobby horse. This was a disappointment. I cannot remember how it was meant to be propelled but I do remember that it refused to move one inch in the mud and rubble that was our back garden. Perhaps it was a hobby mule.

Now here I was in hospital for the second time and in altogether more worrying circumstances. Furthermore, I was approaching sixty, more self-conscious and far less adaptable than I was aged six.

The first thing to go is your dignity. Partly it's the uniform you put on when you get to the ward: a three-quarter length cotton bib, patterned all over with the words 'Hospital Use Only', and tied at the back – if you're lucky – with ribbons.

Along with dignity, however, goes self-consciousness, which I found liberating. We may pretend indifference to our personal appearance, but which of us would not feel mortified to discover, on our return home from a dinner party for example, that our flies had been undone all evening?

After two days on the ward, I was happily strolling through the ward nodding graciously to the visitors clustered round my neighbours' beds, while revealing several yards of bare, spindly leg and wrinkled black underpants. (Some of my colleagues didn't bother with the underpants, so perhaps I did retain some vestige of civilisation}.

I was in a mixed ward with just six beds.

In one corner there was a very grand lady who reminded me of my mother-in-law. She came from Playden. Next to her was John. He liked telling rude jokes despite the fact that he had recently suffered from a heart attack. This upset Lady Playden.

In the other corner was a very old lady who kept mouthing words at me across the room and signalling. She seemed to be in some distress.

On my right on my side of the room was Paul. He was in a very sorry state and was usually curtained off. One could only assess his state of health by the noises that emanated from behind the curtains.

On my left was a younger lady who had just returned from a holiday in the Gambia. She frolicked around in a skimpy nightdress to show off her tan. There did not appear to be much wrong with her. Her boyfriend was called Steve but, judging from the phone calls, he was not altogether reliable. I christened her Hot Pants.

The nurses tried quite hard to make a distinction between night and day, turning out the main lights and lowering their voices, but in fact lights flashed and bleepers bleeped continuously, and there was always someone at your bedside with a blood pressure machine or a needle. Those lucky enough to find sleep were likely to snore.

In addition to the above distractions, I was surprised on my first night to be aroused in the small hours by a truly extraordinary noise emanating from behind the curtain, which sounded like something between the groaning of some very large animal and a fire siren. The nurses were kind and soothing and eventually Paul subsided.

The ward was hot and most of time we dozed, but life was punctuated with little dramas.

Lady Playden liked to summon the nurse regularly. On one occasion she asked, "Am I dead?"

The nurse looked a little flustered and didn't know quite what to say.

"Well, there's nothing registering on the monitor, is there?"

Fortunately, her eyesight was not what it was, and she was still alive. Very much so.

Hot Pants had been given the all-clear and was off home. This made her even more skittish than usual and prompted her to share her life story with the ward. Her husband, who was not Steve, had had an organ transplant, organ unidentified. As a consequence, she was an expert on all things medical. Steve was trying to keep two women, and he couldn't afford it. She was off on another holiday to Turkey. She might give up smoking but did not sound altogether convinced about this. She had been a trained chef from the age of sixteen, so she was off to prepare herself a good meal. On the other hand, she might go out for a few pints and a "Chinesy." Anyway, she was off, and the ward would be a good deal more peaceful as a consequence.

Most of the time there was a tall, handsome black man who sauntered round the wards with a broom. He had a wonderful, dreamy sort of smile, and always said, "Excuse me, sah," as he swept the crumbs and rubbish under the bed.

After lunch a new patient was wheeled in. She looked a little alarming. She had a hanging face like a bloodhound, with two lovely black eyes, and Dickensian tufts of hair that stuck out at angles. From time to time, she pushed her head through the curtain and stared at each of us in turn.

The nurses were wonderfully patient.

"Where am I?"

"You're in hospital, Margot."

"What for?"

"We're going to make you better."

"What for? I'm not ill."

"You had a nasty turn."

"Where am I?" etc.

Later she put her head through the curtain again. "I am from a good home, you know."

At last, I was to have my treatment, an angioplasty. This involved pushing a tube through a vein in my groin, travelling up to the heart and inserting a couple of stents to ease the blockage. The thought of it was a little off-putting but I was told it was entirely painless and so it proved. Later one of Sally's friends wryly observed that the way to a man's heart is through his groin.

After this I was required to lie still for four hours. This was made more difficult by the fact that Margot had called for the commode after what may well have been a considerable period of bowel inactivity. I only survived the event by sucking one of the wine gums the family had brought me and burying my head in a bowl of hyacinths. The situation was not helped by John sitting in his bed on the other side of the room holding his nose and pretending to pull an imaginary chain.

The next day I was allowed home. This was such a relief that it prompted a spirit of complacent compassion which must have been terribly annoying for the rest of the patients. I toured the ward wishing them all well and was a little miffed at the bluntness of their responses.

# Chapter 9

# Rwanda

The problem now was what to do. During our time at the school, we had held a number of training days most of which were wholly forgettable. However, I remember one early on that stood out as it was led by a very inspirational expert. She began by asking whether the school had a motto. When we confessed that we had not, she urged us to create one, suggesting that it might help us to focus our minds on what exactly we were trying to achieve. There was a lot of productive debate and eventually we came up with this. "Pro aliis optimum agree." "To do our best for the benefit of others." We were pleased with it.

Indeed, we created a special badge we awarded to children who demonstrated this commitment, and I think it was cherished. I also like to think it motivated a lot of pupils to lead lives of service and commitment to others.

Now it was time for me to try to earn the badge. I had loved my time at the school, but it was generally quite comfortable. Indeed, Sally's military uncle expressed the opinion that I had never left my mother's womb. This was possibly a little harsh, but it did seem the right moment to take on a stiffer challenge.

Sally suggested Voluntary Service Overseas and we both duly trained. This involved roleplay. We were told to imagine that we had been injured and had to use the only vehicle to travel to the nearest clinic. On arrival we discover a very long queue, especially mothers with children. The doctors see us and immediately beckon us to the front of the queue. What would we do?

Some said they would accept the invitation because they had important work to do and needed to get back. This annoyed the Kenyan on the course who wondered why they thought their work was more important than that of all the other people in the queue. There was no answer to that.

This same Kenyan was offered another scenario. He was working in a very remote village and next door to where he lived there was a very attractive widow. One evening she comes to his door to say that she is lonely. What would he do? The Kenyan grinned widely and declared that he thought he would have won the lotto!

Just as we were completing out training our elder son's wife gave birth to twins and Sally, understandably, said that she no longer wanted to go abroad for two years. I had no such misgivings and was lined up to go and work with the San tribe in Namibia. This was very exciting and involved learning to drive a four-wheel drive vehicle on sand dunes. Unfortunately, the funding for the project fell through and I had to think again.

At this point a couple of former parents who had been working in Rwanda came to tea. We had been supporting their work for many years and they wondered whether I would now be interested in going out to help. This seemed providential. I committed to six months.

# Chapter 10

# Preparations

My briefing was brief. I was to act as Administrator for the Diocese of Cyangugu and be answerable to the bishop. The only piece of advice I was given was not to drive at night.

Sally was immediately into list making mode. I had enough sprays, creams, powders and tablets to eliminate the entire population of mosquitoes in Rwanda, and the wide range of first aid kits, prophylactics, and conventional medications were supported by an equally impressive collection of homeopathic remedies. I just hoped that the immigration authorities would not mistake me for a drug smuggler.

The fact is some of our correspondents had made us nervous. One well-travelled mother told me that she had found a black mamba wrapped round her bath tap one morning and another friend offered a graphic description of trying to kill a scorpion which he discovered under his pillow. They don't squash that easily!

Some of my former pupils tried to be helpful by preparing a First Aid manual for Africa, but I was not altogether convinced by their suggestions. "To remove dust from the eye," I was instructed, "pull the eye down over the nose." "For a nosebleed, put the nose much lower than the body until the heart stops." "For a dog bite, put the dog away for several days. If he has not recovered, then kill it." "For fainting, rub the person's chest or, if a lady, rub her arm instead. Alternatively put the head between the legs of the nearest medical doctor." I think that one might work, but for the fact that there are few local doctors, and they might be rather alarmed to find a newly arrived Englishman adopting such a procedure.

I wondered what I would make of the Rwandans. I knew I would find this a stunningly beautiful country, full of natural wonders:

the mountain-ringed island sea that is Lake Kivu, alongside which nestles the Church Guest House; the immense Nyungwe Forest with its chimpanzees, monkeys and rare birds; the wild savannah of Akagera National Park, and above all, perhaps, some of Africa's most memorable scenery, an endless succession of steep cultivated mountains, interlaced with numerous gurgling rivers and sparkling lakes. The Land of a Thousand Hills.

And the climax to all this would almost certainly be a visit to the Virunga Mountains and *The Gorillas in the Mist*. My guidebook told me that "anybody who has looked into the liquid brown eyes of a wild mountain gorilla will confirm this is quite probably the single most awesome and emotional encounter to be had in a continent known for its peerless wildlife."

And what of the Rwandans? When I told family and friends where I was planning to travel a lot responded by wondering whether that wasn't a bit risky and dangerous.

The horror of the genocide would seem to bear this out but I was assured by those who had visited the country that it was orderly and safe and that the people were, by and large, very friendly.

I was looking forward to getting to know them ...

# Chapter 11

# Landing

I took a night flight to Kigali via Nairobi and Bujumbura, the capital of Burundi for those who want to show off at Trivial Pursuit.

Kigali was teeming. Cars careered down the roads belching smoke and sounding their horns, and beside the dusty roads hundreds of people were walking, apparently in no particular direction and with no particular purpose. By the same token hundreds were hanging around doing nothing very much, perhaps because there really was nothing very much for them to do.

The driver from the diocese in Cyangugu met me at the airport and proved to be a delightfully gentle and patient man called P. Our first mission was to exchange the cash which I had brought from UK under the English bishop's instructions.

The procedure for changing the money was unusual. We went to the ironmongers, of course, where I was casually instructed

to crawl under the counter and into the back room. There sat a clean-cut Asian called Anis with a large computer and an even larger safe. Apparently, he offered the best exchange rate in Kigali and minutes later I was walking out with five million Rwandan francs in a yellow plastic bag. I reflected that this dubious process may have gained the Church a few extra francs, but it was quite possible that someone would hit me over the head and steal the lot. A bank transfer struck me as a rather more sensible option.

The next day I was driven down to Cyangugu in the Church Land Rover. This was so old I had to spend the entire journey clutching the door handle to prevent it from swinging open.

Leaving Kigali was hazardous, because whilst there were many traffic lights, not many of them worked.

Once on the open road things were easier although it seemed to me that the bicycles ought to have commanded greater respect than they did. They carried the most phenomenal loads, anything from milk churns to sacks of wheat, doors, corrugated tin sheets and vast bundles of wood. I counted 63 yellow plastic water carriers on one bike.

The bicycles were mainly of the old Raleigh upright design, and they had no gears. And Rwanda is a land of a thousand hills.

Uphill, the struggle must have been painfully backbreaking, although some cyclists eased the problem by hanging on to the backs of lorries, a procedure which I felt sure would have met with Sally's disapproval.

The downhill run was frankly alarming. The bikes and their loads flew down the hills without the slightest chance of being able to stop in an emergency.

The procedure for approaching towns and villages involved clearing the roads by sounding the horn continuously and increasing your speed. This was remarkably effective, although the crowds of pedestrians and cyclists had refined the art of waiting to leave the road until the very last second, so that if you were new to the game, like me, the whole thing was a hair-raising experience.

The drive through the forest was breathtakingly beautiful. The mountains were bathed in a gentle blue mist, and occasionally we saw little black and white monkeys hopping about the verges and bushes.

We arrived safely at Kamembe, the principal town of Cyangugu, and made for the Peace Guest House where I was to stay for my six months. I was delighted to find that I was to be accommodated in a spacious rondavel with spectacular views across Lake Kivu.

The next day I decided to take a walk to the airport snack bar for lunch. The airport was the first to be built in Rwanda but could only accommodate smallish planes as there was a big hill at the end of the runway. The whole place had a rather rundown, derelict feel about it, and I suspect that the armed guards at the entrance were serving no useful purpose. Apparently, there were no flights in or out, perhaps because of the unrest in Bukavu, just across the border in the Congo.

Still, there was a snack bar, so I was happy to order a Fanta and an omelette for lunch. The Fanta (warm) arrived quite quickly, but it was an hour or so before the lady of the house appeared to explain that there was a problem. They had no eggs. I settled for a goat brochette instead. Chewy.

My first forays into the town were somewhat unnerving. I was not the only white person there, but certainly there were very few, and you did feel very much in a minority: a lot of the people stared at you; some begged, although this was not persistent or aggressive; a few threw derisory comments, and some shouted friendly greetings.

Overwhelmingly I was struck by the desperate poverty: women sat with a dozen tiny, silver fish laid out on a cloth for sale and all covered with flies: the whole lot might have fetched 10p, but none appeared to have been sold; there was a man with legs too weak and thin to carry him, who was literally crawling along the street on his hands and knees.

A curious mixture of emotions was stirred: there was unease – might they turn on me and steal my wallet; there was admiration – how could they remain so cheerful in the face of such abject poverty?: there was pity, because while there were many who were cheerful, there were some whose eyes registered only hopelessness and despair; and, of course, there was guilt – what right had I to be enjoying such a totally disproportionately indulgent lifestyle?

Whilst we had travelled down P and I had had plenty of opportunity to chat. He told me that he had three lovely daughters and that his wife was expecting another baby which he secretly hoped would be a boy.

Imagine our delight when, weeks later, the wife went into labour and gave birth to a little boy, However, there were complications.

We had some American medics staying at the Guest House at the time who were working with an organisation called "Feed my Lambs". Three of them were at the hospital when this crisis occurred, and they did their best to help.

They returned to the Guest House after 24 hours weary and ashen faced. The little boy had died.

They told me that there was no blood for the mother and no oxygen for the baby. Their assessment of the hospital was a blunt one: "a dead loss". It was probably too harsh a judgement as the mother did pull through, which would almost certainly not have been the case had she been in one of the villages, but the fact is that the hospital is working with desperately limited facilities.

The funeral took place the next day.

It was extremely moving. P's three little girls, aged seven, five and three, led their baby brother to his grave carrying a simple wooden cross. P was heartbroken, but towards the end of the service he stood up to speak. "I just want to say two things," he said, "first I want to thank the American nurses for helping to give our little boy 24 hours of life. I also want you to know that we have decided to call our son Hope."

Afterwards we shared a Fanta in P's house with all his friends and family. There wasn't a lot to say, so we just held hands and prayed and wept for the pity of it all.

# Chapter 12

# Admin

So here I was, the new Administrator for the Diocese, commonly known as Admin, a soubriquet that has stayed with me long after I gave up the work.

My office was situated next to the building known as the cathedral. The name may well conjure up a misleading image for you, because the cathedral was a large rectangular brick building with a tin roof and no architectural merit at all.

I had not really understood what the admin job involved but it turned out that for six months I was to take on the responsibility for the Church finances and at the end of that period appoint someone to carry on that role.

This was a huge undertaking. I was to be responsible for issuing invoices, paying all the bills and salaries and keeping all the accounts. As the diocese had well over thirty churches, two private schools, a carpentry workshop, a guest house and a farm there was quite a lot to do. However, what made it really challenging was that there was never enough money. Furthermore, the bishop had a curiously cavalier approach to the problem. He had a number of cars, the favourite being an old Range Rover which had been brought over from UK. It was almost certainly the only one of its kind in the country so spare parts were hard to find and enormously expensive. I used to dread him coming into the office to demand two million Rwandan francs for the garage. When I explained that we didn't have two million francs he would waft the problem away. "Don't pay the staff for a couple of months," he suggested. "God will provide." It occurred to me that God's solution and the bishop's might not coincide.

Staff pay bothered me anyway. A guard received the princely sum of a thousand francs a month, equivalent to ten pounds, was not a living wage even in Rwanda. There was one exception to this. It was the bishop's guard who was paid twice the amount. When I questioned this, I was told it was because the guard worked day and night.

Income was paltry. A church might raise ten pounds a month from the collections. The farm made a loss because it had to give most of the milk from the cows to the bishop and the carpentry workshop also struggled because the furniture it made for the diocese was rarely paid for. The only organisations that made money were the private schools so I had to insist that they make a monthly contribution to the diocese. Understandably this was resented.

There was a lot to adjust to.

This was largely a cash economy. Indeed, there was probably quite a large proportion of the population who did not even run to cash but survived by barter. However, most of our bills had to be paid in cash, so I found myself regularly visiting the bank and withdrawing millions of Rwandan francs.

At a glance, the banks appeared quite efficient, with the smartest buildings in town and rows of computers. This was deceptive. To withdraw cash, you were required to approach a large lady who was enthroned in a glass booth. There was always a long queue, because all bank employees had been carefully trained to work as slowly as possible and with as much indifference as they could muster.

Upon reaching the booth, the lady studiously ignored you for a couple of minutes, and then picked up your cheque, eyeing it suspiciously as though it might possibly explode. Eventually she sniffed and passed it through the little hatch by her side.

Here there sat a man who appeared to do nothing all day but peer at an empty computer screen. He too ignored your cheque for a few minutes, then fished around for it with an outstretched hand, and sauntered across to the other side of the bank to hand it to another man who was also staring at an empty screen.

The second man received the cheque with indifference. In the meantime, the large lady had left her booth to join the two men with the cheque. A long discussion ensued, interspersed with suspicious glances in my direction, so that, on the first occasion this happened, I began to think I must have done something wrong. But no. This was the normal procedure, and eventually the lady dawdled back to her booth and counted out your money in enormous wodges.

The whole procedure was so excruciatingly tedious, that I was often tempted to do something outrageous. Then I would remember that the guards outside carried guns.

The diocese was not run very efficiently. For some reason the drivers were paid three times what a teacher earned even though a lot of the time they had nothing to do. One of the drivers was called Ph. He was the Del boy of Cyangugu. He spoke very broken English and was very good at smiling in a winning sort of way.

When Sally came out to visit, she decided to take Ph in hand. Anyone who knew Ph would be amazed at the transformation. Indeed, for one brief moment, he was seen to break into a trot. He was also persuaded to start painting the new manager's house at the farm. When the time comes for us to take stock of our time in Rwanda, this may well go down as our finest achievement.

Mind you, Ph made a dreadful fuss. At the end of the first day of this new departure in his life, he arrived in the office, covered from head to foot in paint, and full of woe. "Nobody help me!" "Velly tired." "Nobody help me!" "Velly high. Sometimes you hit down." "Nobody help me!"

"I go home."

Sally did go and hold his ladder the next day but, despite this, he managed to fall off and was on sick leave for three weeks.

I found myself having regular run-ins with the bishop. Our two offices were opposite each other, and I noticed that folk used to sit outside for days waiting to see the bishop. I suggested he had a diary giving people fixed appointments so that they didn't have to waste their time waiting for him. He brushed this aside. "They don't mind waiting for me. They're used to waiting."

Occasionally we would travel to the parishes together. These were often remote and involved hours of bouncing along muddy, rock-strewn tracks. Once we came to a particularly perilous bridge. Before crossing, I suggested that the bishop might pray for us. Instead, he got out, watched as we drove across the bridge and then rejoined us on the other side.

On another occasion, this time without the bishop, we were driving through the forest when we encountered a massive tree that had fallen across the track. There were about thirty men and women there with their machetes, but they were not making much impression. However, they assured us they would have it clear within a couple of hours, so we sat and waited.

As we waited what passed for an ambulance appeared from the other side. As we were on the town and hospital side of the obstacle we offered to turn round and take the patient. Surprisingly the offer was refused with no explanation.

Hours later there was no sign of the tree being moved so we decided to go back anyway: a night in the forest in a car was very much to be avoided.

As we made to go, the ambulance driver leapt over the tree and asked us to take his patient. We agreed, of course, and were at a loss to understand why he had refused our earlier offer.

The patient was a young lady. She was manhandled over the tree and bundled onto the back seat of our pick-up. We asked what the problem was.

"Oh, she's having a baby and it's a breach birth. One foot out. No more."

We were horrified. Why had there been no sense of urgency?

The journey back was tense. We felt every bump and jolt, but not a sound issued from the patient. At times I wondered whether she had died.

We did eventually reach the hospital, the baby was safely born and the mother survived. Hallelujah!

Life in my Rondavel was not altogether uneventful. One night I discovered the largest spider I have ever seen scuttling across my bedroom wall. Normally I would call upon Sally in situations like these, but there being no Sally there was no option but to deal with the situation myself. I did toy briefly with the idea of simply hiding under the bed covers, but then I began to imagine the hairy monster might be lonely and curious and want someone with whom to cuddle up. No, it had to go.

The simple technique of trapping it under a glass, sliding a postcard across and depositing it outside was not going to work for the simple reason that the spider was too big – at least four inches in diameter – well three. I might have used my sun hat, but its straw was wearing thin, and it offered too many opportunities for escape. So, I decided instead to catch it in my sponge bag.

Operation entrapment worked remarkably successfully. Perhaps lured by the enticing aroma of my Palmolive aftershave, the unsuspecting creature crawled in quietly, unwisely feeling this was a pleasant place to settle down for the night. Hey presto! A quick tug on the two cords, and the job was done.

After all this drama I slept but fitfully, waking early and itching all over. Do spiders bite?

A shower was needed.

Unfortunately, I had been without hot water for two weeks. Plumbers, it would seem, were as hard to come by in Rwanda as they are in UK. We did find one fellow who claimed to have the necessary expertise. He arrived with a single spanner, loosened what he thought was the offending bolt, and unleashed the entire contents of the tank to flood the bathroom floor. The man quickly disappeared and has not been seen since.

So, my early morning shower had to be taken in Rondavel 4.

We had a new night guard at the Guest House. Normally night guards spend the night asleep, but this fellow was new and keen. Imagine his excitement when he saw a shadowy, scantily attired figure scampering down the path. He straddled the path, shone his flashlight in my direction, and shouted a few incomprehensible phrases which sounded distinctly unfriendly.

And in this hour of crisis, of course, my newly acquired Kinyarwanda failed me. Why hadn't I learned the words for shower, plumber and spider?

By now the assiduous guard had allowed his flashlight to wander, enabling him to establish that he had in fact accosted a mazungu. As the realization dawned on him, aggression melted into embarrassment, and I was allowed to proceed clutching my towel along with the few shreds of dignity which I had left.

However, I did need a clean start because we had a synod meeting that morning. To be honest, I had no idea what a synod meeting was, but it sounded important, and the bishop had been doing an awful lot of letter writing, photo copying and fussing, so I felt as though I needed to make an effort. Indeed, for the first time in my year in Rwanda I planned to wear a suit!

So here I was, spick and span, and looking altogether more like Admin. I made a point of greeting the new guard as I passed the office, and I rather think he gave me a knowing wink! What did he think I had been up to?

There was another occasion when my dignity as the Diocesan Admin was very nearly compromised.

Most of the time the church guest house was empty, but there was an occasional influx of earnest evangelicals, intent on planting churches and saving souls. One weekend the guest house found itself overbooked, and in an act of quite remarkable self-sacrifice, I offered to vacate my rondavel and move into the Hotel de Chutes for the weekend. You will appreciate that the fact that I found evangelicals very tiresome company and the Hotel de Chutes served ice cold Mutzig beer had nothing to do with the decision.

No sooner had I vacated my rondavel, than the "girls" moved in to give it a once over. Imagine their surprise/delight/horror when from the bottom of Admin's wardrobe, they unearthed two pairs of extremely skimpy knickers. Indeed, when the lady in charge of rooms came to report the discovery, she was the closest an African can become to blushing.

There was an innocent explanation for all this, dear reader.

Two visiting ladies had been very impressed with our work and took a particular shine to an orphan girl called Violet. When the ladies departed, they left money to buy Violet a new dress. I delegated the purchase to a lady in my team and she returned not just with a dress but also with the two pairs of knickers. I am ashamed to say that whilst I was happy to give the orphan girl the new dress, I drew the line at gifting the knickers and hid them in my cupboard instead. Honestly.

# Chapter 13

# Church Services

As Admin I felt it was my duty to attend church each Sunday. My first service lasted three hours, eleven minutes and forty-two seconds, not that I was timing it.

The service began with all eighty visitors introducing themselves individually, a procedure made more protracted by the fact that each introduction was hailed with a loud fanfare from the electronic organ. This produced an unusual range of sounds including bird song, a drum roll, what sounded like the squealing of brakes, and most extraordinary of all, a man with a rather manic laugh. For one terrible, nightmarish moment I felt sure that they were going to haul me up to the front to introduce myself, and follow this with the fellow laughing, setting off the entire congregation. Mercifully I was spared.

I lost count, but I think there were six choirs. I liked the children's choir best: they had one little fellow banging a drum for all he was worth, and with an unerring sense of rhythm. He was having a wonderful time.

The choir from Butare were pretty good too, clapping and swaying and smiling in a very winning way, but their songs did seem to have an awful lot of verses.

There followed the prayers. These started quite calmly, but gradually gathered momentum and intensity, so that the whole thing resembled a Peter O'Sullevan commentary on a rather long horse race with a very close finish and "Hallelujah" as the winner.

Next, we had the sermon to look forward to. Unfortunately, at this point the bishop's son, Sam, moved himself alongside me and offered to translate. This was unwelcome as it meant I had to try to keep awake. We began with lengthy greetings and were then into the meat of the matter. If I understood it correctly, we started with Jesus stilling the storm, and then moved on to the sinking of the Titanic, which basically went down because Jesus was not on board.

As the Titanic was taking a long time to sink, there was time to ponder this thesis, and I wondered whether, in truth, Jesus can, or should, be relied upon to save us from disasters: perhaps rather he can be depended upon to help us to cope with them in the best possible way. I was mulling over this thought in a rather dreamy sort of way as the heat began to build up under the metal roof of the cathedral in the midday sun, and I am ashamed to record that I fell sound asleep. Suddenly Sam gave me a nudge which was not far off a poke. The preacher was introducing his second text for the day. This was from Ephesians 5, and read:

> Wake up, O sleeper,
> Rise from the dead ...

What's more the minister clearly intended to put our faith to the test, because he spoke for a further forty-five minutes on the subject.

Eventually the glorious moment arrived when Sam gave me another poke and intimated that we were reaching the conclusion.

Perhaps now a closing hymn, a blessing and lunch? After all, it was well past midday.

Not a bit of it. It was time for confessions, and there was a real stir of interest in the congregation. We were treated to a lurid collection of sins, quite a lot to do with drinking, I am afraid, and I just counted my blessings that we have not yet introduced this practice at my local church at Mountfield. I prefer my conscience to be a matter between myself and the Almighty.

Indeed, the whole service was not quite my style, but there was a certain spontaneity and openness and joyfulness about it all, and I do not wish my commentary in any way to be taken as disrespectful: I write with affection, not scorn. I am quite sure that the Rwandans would find our worship strange and amusing – and so very solemn!

## Chapter 14

# Humanitarian Work

The main mission of the Church was to evangelise and plant churches. This was fine but any time and energy I had left after wrestling with the accounts and the bishop, I wanted to devote to trying to help the poor.

My first challenge was to use the money that the prep school had raised through the immense generosity of parents and friends to build two dormitories. A local secondary school had 400 boarding girls with nowhere to sleep but the classrooms. I did wonder how on earth you would settle down in a dormitory with 200 teenage girls, but it was not for me to ask questions like that.

It took some persuasion but eventually the bishop agreed to a scheme whereby we undertook to help ten of the poorest families in each parish each year. Whilst I had my doubts about the Church hierarchy, I have to say that, rather in the mould of Chaucer's poor parson, many of the parish priests were outstanding, dedicated to the well-being of the people in their care. I loved working with them, identifying and supporting the most desperate families.

Occasionally I stayed the night in a village at the priest's house. This was an education. All year round it is dark by 6 p.m. and as there is no electricity it's early to bed. The problem with this is that it means at least one visit to the loo during the night. The loo is located outside, of course, and it is necessary to negotiate the livestock to reach it. The loo consisted of a simple hole in the ground with none of the additional facilities to which one has become accustomed – no loo paper, no wash-hand basin, no Air-Wick. It was necessary to improvise, but, goodness, don't you appreciate things properly when you have to do without them, if only for a night.

Some of the early people we helped were suffering from the aftermath of the genocide.

The Rwandan government is determined to remember the genocide and to do all that it can to avoid such a thing ever happening again. Each year a week is devoted to remembering the genocide and there are memorials scattered all over the country with the mantra, "Never again."

A visit to the genocide memorial at Shangi is a sobering experience. It is one of sixty such memorials in Rwanda and is sited beside a large Catholic church where 80,000 Tutsis took shelter, were initially besieged and starved of food and water by the Interahamwe, and then brutally slaughtered. The memorial is held in a small underground building filled with coffins and lined with shelves that are packed with bones and skulls, many of them fractured. There is one complete skeleton, hunched up and partially clothed. There are also large plastic bags full of bloodstained clothes. It is grim.

There appear to be few visitors but there are a dozen or so widows who are keeping vigil and remembering the dead.

We then pass through the large courtyard of the neighbouring school to the remains of the cesspit where most of the bodies were initially slung.

There is a stillness in the air. One of the ladies volunteers to speak: she herself was one of the victims and was thrown into the pit. Miraculously she survived, but she lost her entire family, husband, two children, mother, father, brothers and sisters. She suddenly bends over to show us the horrendous scars on her head and body. She says that she survived the siege by cutting herself and drinking her own blood, and later she pretended to be dead. It was only because it was raining torrentially that a few were left alive. The Red Cross eventually rescued her. Now she says the mental scars are worse than the physical ones, and she is finding it very difficult to rebuild her life.

Up till then, I had mainly avoided the subject of the genocide, but once the people begin to talk about it there is no stopping them. The catalogue of horror and atrocity tumbles out, and I think that the Rwandans themselves can hardly believe what has happened or begin to explain how or why. There were some evil instigators and ringleaders, of course, but many who participated were "normal", known neighbours.

Much has been written about the genocide by people who know much more than me. All I can do here is to tell two personal stories that I encountered as part of our humanitarian programme and each of which, interestingly enough, matches the horror of it all with great courage and heroism.

V was a widow from the genocide. Indeed, she lost her husband and all eight children. She lived in a mud house with a tin roof. The walls were full of holes, some stuffed pathetically with bits of plastic. She survived by digging in the fields for 20p per day.

When I first met V she hardly spoke at all and found it difficult to look you in the eyes.

"When I see the poverty of my life, and when I think of my husband and children, I find that my life is a living death."

We were able to do a little for V: we built her a new wooden house, we bought her a couple of goats and, most important of all, we found her an orphan girl to care for. Later I took a friend to visit her. She welcomed us with a smile and a warm embrace. She took us into her house and shut all the doors and windows so that we were in complete darkness. The experience was made a little more alarming because there were little creatures scuttling around our feet. Daylight later revealed these to be guinea pigs, a regular supply of Sunday lunches.

In the darkness V prayed. The prayer was long and intense and there were lots of it that I did not understand. However, the unmistakable burden of the prayer was to thank God for all her blessings.

When we first met F, she was living in absolute poverty: her little house was dark and dingy, and she had no running water, yet she took great pride in her appearance, and was beautifully turned out. She, and a number of her friends, accompanied us on our visits to all the orphans, taking real pleasure in our shared delight with the pigs we had given them and their makeshift sties.

Communication was not easy, but the Africans love singing, so as we slithered along the narrow paths, Sally and I tried a verse of *Give me love in my heart keep me serving* so that they could all join in the chorus of hosannas. That worked well, and soon we were experimenting with a few of their choruses, and the girls were giggling with delight at our feeble attempts at Kinyarwanda. We spent a very happy afternoon together: they were full of warmth and gratitude, and their simple courage and generous hearts were far more precious gifts than anything we had to offer. Anyway, it was all a powerful antidote to the rows of skulls.

F lost her mother in the genocide, along with other members of her family, when she was just twelve-years-old. Since then, she has brought up her two brothers, G and M, aged eight and six at the time.

The struggle to bring up her family in the aftermath of this has been long and difficult, made worse by the fact that the men who did the killing have constantly returned to taunt and threaten her. Indeed, as the Gacaca courts approached it seems they killed Francine's pig as a warning of what might happen to her if she dared to speak out.

There was one moment which particularly struck us in Francine's testimony. It was when she was describing how the men came to taunt and threaten her. She added, almost in passing, "If only they would come and say that they were sorry, I think that I would have it in my heart to forgive them."

# Chapter 15

# The Farm

There was little employment in rural Rwanda and most of the people in our area survived on subsistence farming. They were also inefficient farmers! For centuries this has not mattered much, as plentiful sunshine and rain had provided plentiful food. However, as the population has grown to the extent that Rwanda is now one of the most densely populated of all African countries, the land struggled to feed its people.

It was in this context that we set out to develop agricultural skills, seeing it as one of the most obvious and immediate ways of helping people to help themselves.

To this end we created a demonstration farm to promote good practice in livestock care, soil improvement and care of the environment. This included a residential training centre with groups of farmers regularly attending.

The site was a beautiful one, high up on a hillside overlooking Kamembe and Bukavu further afield, with spectacular views all round. It was only a small farm of about eight hectares.

At the beginning the farm was very rundown. The land was poor, the livestock old and unproductive and the manager dishonest.

It took us a long while to address these issues and if I am honest, the farm never became a profitable operation. However, we did train hundreds of farmers most of whom reported back to say that their training had led to greater success which in turn had brought three key benefits: they ate better, they could afford the uniform, shoes and equipment necessary to enable their children to attend school, and they could afford basic health insurance.

We experimented with different crops and livestock, often unsuccessfully.

As the local hens were remarkably unproductive, we decided to buy some Ugandan chickens from Kigali. It was a long day! After a six-hour drive it took us some time to find the supplier, and then the chickens were not packed and ready for collection. Furthermore, we had to construct a makeshift shade for the back as it was a blisteringly hot day, and we were convinced that the birds would all expire. In the event we reached the farm after dark, exhausted but with every single chick alive and kicking.

The celebrations were short lived. It was Bunwell all over again. Quite quickly the birds started to die, first in their ones and twos, then more rapidly. I began to dread visiting the farm! It transpired in the end that the chicks were suffering from Marek's disease against which they had not been inoculated. We lost about thirty per cent of the flock, so it was not a complete disaster, but it has not been possible to continue as the Government has placed a ban on importing birds since the outbreak of bird flu.

Pigs and goats did better. Rwandan goats are very hardy, but they produce little milk and the Rwandans are not keen to drink the little milk they do produce. This is "cultural", I was told. Nevertheless we planned to introduce dairy goats from Uganda, and thought we might persuade AIDS sufferers to keep them as the milk is very nutritious, just what they need if they are to cope with antiretroviral drugs.

The pigs were a great success. We developed extensive sties and boasted some of the largest pigs I have seen in Rwanda. They were mainly fed on the leftovers from the schools which seemed to suit them well.

However, we had problems importing a suitable boar. We discovered that the Pastor at Banda had managed to rear a particularly fine fellow, and, in the interests of economy, we decided to collect him ourselves. Have you ever tried to load a full-size boar into the back of a pick-up van?

The operation started well. The large fellow trundled out of his pen in a good-natured fashion and happily followed the trail of sweet potatoes which led to the vehicle. It was only when he was a few feet away that he sensed danger, especially as a big crowd of men, women and children were closing in behind him. Suddenly he turned, and with a banshee howl of fury charged at us all in a frenzy of indignation. We scattered in terror.

It was time to regroup and rethink our strategy. Clearly this pig was too smart to be lured into the van, so brute force was the only answer. The trouble was that the brute force of twenty or so men was no match for the brute force of Napoleon. With men hanging on to his ears, tail, legs and any other grabbable bit, he still managed to squeal and lash with such power that our resolve faltered. Indeed, it was a miracle that none of us lost an arm or a leg.

It took the best part of an hour to wear him down, and even when we had managed to bundle him into the van and tie his legs together, he still made one last desperate bid for freedom.

It was pitch black by the time we reached Murangi Farm, but at least our pig now seemed resigned to his lot. Perhaps it was the prospect of enjoying the left-over food from the local school which persuaded him that the move may not be such a bad one.

Apart from completing the two dormitories, we attracted funds to build new classrooms and organised teacher training in the holidays, mainly using volunteers from UK. The Rwandan Government decided, for good reason, to switch from using French as the second language and the medium for teaching to English. The problem was that, instead of phasing it over a period, it was decided it must be done at a stroke, and this despite the fact that many of the teachers had little or no English.

We did what we could to help but a generation of schoolchildren suffered as a consequence of this hasty decision, and there is still work to be done.

For some reason Rwandans all seem to muddle r's and l's when speaking English. We were confused early on when the accounts had an entry of 500 francs for a rock for the accountant's desk. Later, when we built a Rondavel at the Alivera (or Arivela) Village, our construction manager persisted in calling it the Land Rover.

More embarrassing was the lesson we once observed. A pupil had come up with a particularly brilliant answer, and the teacher exclaimed, "Well done! That's vely good answer. Let's give him a good crap. Come on, everybody, crap together."

## Chapter 16

# Shooting Dogs

The truth is that life in Cyangugu could be rather dreary and uneventful, and at times even a little depressing.

As you can imagine, it was with some relief that I cadged a lift up to Kigali. By a remarkable coincidence one of the former parents at the school I ran was in Kigali producing a film about the genocide called *Shooting Dogs*. She was desperate for some extras and, needless to say, I jumped at the opportunity.

The film is set in a mission school in Kigali, where 3,500 Tutsis took shelter but were eventually abandoned by the French and UN soldiers to be slaughtered by their Hutu neighbours.

The film is powerful and grueling. At one point the Tutsis plead with the leader of the UN soldiers to shoot them before they leave knowing that this will be a better death than one waiting for them at the hands of the Hutus. When the leader refuses, they ask whether they at least would shoot the children.

The scene in which I appeared involved the evacuation of the Europeans from the school. Three or four lorries roar into the school, we all jump into the backs of them and off we go. Outside the gates are hundreds of Rwandan extras playing the Hutus waiting the departure of the UN with their sharpened machetes.

We arrived early in the morning for the first take but there followed at least another ten takes during the day.

What was concerning was that the number of Hutus outside the school increased steadily during the course of the day, as did the menace and hysteria with which they screamed and waved their machetes. By the end of the day the line between make-believe and reality became frighteningly blurred.

Why *Shooting Dogs?* The UN soldiers were instructed only to shoot if they were shot at. The Tutsis are puzzled, then, when they hear the soldiers shooting outside the school. When they return the Tutsi leader asks the leader why his soldiers are shooting. The UN leader explains that they were shooting the dogs that were devouring the bodies.

It is an episode in history of which the powers behind the United Nations should be ashamed. If they had simply ordered the taking of the radio stations much of the slaughter could have been prevented.

The day after the film shooting I had to return to Cyangugu in one of those wretched Okapi buses which left, as I thought, at seven a.m.. Knowing these buses fill up quickly, I arrived in good time, only to discover that it was due to leave at eight. Nothing daunted, I loaded my case into the boot, and went off in search of breakfast. It would appear that by and large the Africans don't bother with this meal.

I was back a good hour before departure and took my place in the back seat as the bus was already filling up. For the next hour it continued to fill up. Just when you thought that really must be it, another large family would arrive, and we would all squeeze up still tighter. I reckoned the bus was designed for fifteen, and we ended up with very nearly double that number.

There then began the most frightening journey I have ever experienced. The man drove like a maniac, going round bends so fast that it was a miracle we stayed on the road, and operating all overtaking manoeuvres as though he were determined to drive the offending obstacle off the road.

By and large the African passengers seemed to take this in their stride, but after half an hour the little girl in front of me turned round, opened the window beside me and attempted to be sick out of it. Unfortunately, she missed.

After an hour or so we stopped for the driver to have a pee and were besieged by vendors insistently sticking their wares through the window: you have to be especially wary of the goat kebabs which are skewered to unpleasantly sharp sticks.

However, what is really upsetting is that the locals tend to use this occasion to take in their weekly supply of meat, and I think we took on board three legs of goat, two skinned rabbits and a chicken. This is all very well, but the Rwandans clearly enjoy their meat "high" so that Admin was obliged to spend the rest of the journey with his head hanging out of the window.

There was only one more stop in this five-hour journey, and at first sight there was no apparent reason for it. We were in the middle of the forest when we screeched to a halt and reversed frantically for a hundred yards. All the passengers were peering excitedly out of the window, and I could only guess that they might have seen some monkeys, or perhaps something even more exotic than that. I allowed myself to be disgorged from the bus and joined my brothers and sisters who were pointing enthusiastically down the steep ravine beside the road. The object of their interest was a bus, not dissimilar from ours, which was lying on its roof smashed to smithereens. It was generally and cheerfully agreed that all but one of the passengers had been killed.

Vainly, I hoped this might have a sobering effect on our driver, but we completed the journey at breakneck speed, only to dawdle through Kamembe for threequarters of an hour before pulling into the bus depot. I arrived back at the Guest House shaken and exhausted, only to discover that my digital camera, no Sally's digital camera, which she had so generously and anxiously lent to me, had been stolen from my bag, doubtless whilst I was in search of breakfast. It was a low point.

# Chapter 17

# Christmas

Just outside our town there was a large refugee camp housing 2,000 Banya Malengi from Bukavu across the border in DRC. This was a race which had strong links with Tutsis in Rwanda, and which had increasingly been pressured out of their homes in the Congo, despite the fact that many of them have lived there for generations. "You are Rwandans. Go home".

Conditions in the camp were grim. There was drinking water and basic sanitation, but not much else. I am reminded of King Lear's agonised cry, *"The basest beggar is in the poorest thing superfluous."* These people seemed to have nothing to spare. They were crowded into huge, hangar-like tents, which had been subdivided into compartments to accommodate three or four families at a time. The tents were just about waterproof, but they offered next to no privacy, and I imagine the noise at night, especially of babies crying, must have been terrible. It would also have been very cold. There seemed to be enough food to prevent starvation, but no more, and cooking was done over open fires.

There were some large "school" tents for teaching the six or seven hundred children. Each tent was empty, except for a blackboard.

I was especially struck by the children. Most were dressed in rags and were very dirty.

They had crowded round the car when we arrived and were full of curiosity: I would guess they were between the ages of four and ten. All wanted to touch or shake hands, and one was especially persistent in this respect. We discovered that he was there without his mother and father who were still "at home".

After my first visit to the camp I came away feeling quite distressed and distraught. I know there had been countless images of starving children in even worse circumstances than the ones I have described, but I found seeing it first-hand had an enormous impact. I shall never forget the sadness in that little boy's eyes, and his gentle, generous, hesitant smile. It was enough to break your heart.

An hour on the verandah at the Rondavel was restorative. I loved looking out across the lake in the morning, hearing the fishermen singing as they brought in their catches. And I loved watching the beautiful, colourful birds flitting amongst the trees and bushes in the morning sunlight. This was the world as God meant it to be.

I became a regular visitor to the refugee camp. Strictly speaking this was a transit camp, too rudimentary and too close to the border to serve as anything else. Nevertheless, since the ethnic cleansing of the Banya Malengi tribe and the mass exodus from the Congo, there had been some three thousand refugees "housed" in the camp, many of them children.

The bishop's advice was to steer well clear of the camp. They are used to living like that, he explained. Perhaps a little foolishly I ignored his advice.

The children loved games. Taking a leaf out of Sally's book, I taught them all the Hokey Kokey, and they also enjoyed a version of grandmother's Footsteps, whereby they tiptoed silently behind me waiting for me to spin round and growl like an ogre. This made them squeal with hysterical delight. Meanwhile the grown-ups looked on with a faint air of disapproval. This was not the way Mazungus were meant to behave.

Looking ahead to Christmas, I decided to give every child at the camp between the ages of three and ten a Christmas stocking. I reckoned I would need five hundred! I found two large sacks of woollen teddies in the container sent from UK, and some American friends left me a huge bag of goodies which they were happy for me to use. With some careful shopping locally, and the addition of many gifts which generous visitors had left behind, I thought I would be able to provide each stocking with a cuddly animal, a ball, a sweet and a pencil and pad of paper.

Sunday was one of the saddest and most disheartening days for me since I arrived in Cyangugu – a day for the cynics to say "We told you so."

Three times I had visited the camp to check with the leaders that they had a system in place for the orderly distribution. They assured me there would be no problem and I had no fewer than six friends to help.

It was chaos. From the moment we arrived we were besieged by children, the stronger ones fighting their way to the front. We were situated inside an enclosure but the children broke through the entrance and climbed over the sides: some even slit the tent material so that they could grab the stockings from the bags.

The adults and "leaders" from the camp were no help. They shouted and argued, in total disarray as to how things should be organised. Many parents pushed ahead with children on their backs, screaming and begging. Then the men started to hit the children with sticks to try to contain them.

At one stage things did calm down a bit and we were able to distribute some of the presents, but this did not last long, and by the end the situation was becoming dangerous for all concerned. All we could do was beat a hasty retreat with the people mobbing the car.

So there was no touching, heart-warming picture of a child clutching its stocking with delight. The only pictures I could have shown you would be of tearing, screaming, fighting, grabbing and weeping, but the camera had been stolen anyway.

It was a sad day. There was no doubt that in my naivete I had only succeeded in adding to the misery and suffering. It was a classic case of a well-meaning but misguided "do-gooder" getting things totally wrong.

Later I went back to discuss with the leaders whether they might be able to distribute things more effectively themselves, without me there. They were angry with me, and full of recrimination. I also noticed that several of them had the biros which had been in the children's stockings proudly attached to their breast pockets.

I arrived home covered in dirt, feeling emotionally and physically drained. I suppose it was a case of "picking up, dusting down, and starting all over again". At any rate, perhaps I was a little wiser.

In many ways we escaped the heavy commercialism of Christmas in Rwanda, but sadly a bit of tackiness was creeping in. We had flashing lights outside the Guest House, and what's worse a horrid little bleeper which played *Jingle Bells* endlessly so that I was tempted to snip the wire. The cathedral was decorated with lights and tinsel, and, if you can believe it, the speakers were blasting out *"I'm Dreaming of a White Christmas"* before the service on Christmas Day. Dream on!

The service itself was long and noisy. For me, the high spot was undoubtedly the nativity play that Sally had previously prepared with the children. Their English was very limited so the play depended heavily on nursery rhymes The stable was packed with farmyard animals, all making the appropriate noises, and the shepherds were greeted with *Baa Baa Black Sheep.* Then, when Jesus was born, the children broke into, *"The sun has got its hat on, hip hip hooray …"*

Christmas lunch was a bit touch and go. We had been promised a turkey, but it didn't arrive till mid-morning, and then it hobbled in on its Zimmer frame. Once cooked, it proved to be mainly skin and bones, and I am afraid it was not greatly enhanced by my efforts with bread sauce and gravy – both were cold and lumpy. Still, we shared it with the staff of the Guest House, and they were very appreciative. After lunch we took lots of photographs, and they all became quite skittish!! And we'd only been drinking Fanta.

After that I took a walk by the lake, which I somehow feel was rather better for my soul than the morning service. Then I sat down to a bit of TV. There now, I hadn't meant to let that slip! I had been keeping quiet about the fact that we had TV, because it didn't really fit with the deprived and pioneer image I had been studiously cultivating. It is true that the TV only worked occasionally and unfortunately it was controlled from the restaurant. The two favourite channels were a daily drama series which always seemed to involve a man drinking too much and being unkind to his wife, or, worse still, the God channel. If I wanted to watch a football match in my room it was necessary to bribe the man who had control of the dib-dabber, and bribing is illegal in Rwanda.

# Chapter 18

# Rwanda Aid

If I am honest, I was glad to finish my six-month stint as Admin, especially as I had found a very capable successor. He was called Richard and had been running the refugee camp with great compassion and care. He was a far better accountant than me. He now works for the Red Cross.

It was also good to be home and to see more of the children and grandchildren. One of my friends had likened my involvement in Rwanda to that of Mrs Jellyby and her "telescopic philanthropy" in *Bleak House*. In her mission to care for the children of Africa, her own children were horribly neglected.

I was troubled by this comparison, not only because I thought there might be some truth in it, but also because I recalled that Mrs Jellyby's Borrioboola-Gha project failed after the local king sold the project's volunteers into slavery in order to buy rum.

So, I determined to give more time to the growing number of grandchildren. This was largely very enjoyable but did also present some challenges. On one occasion we were required to look after the twins aged six. As bedtime approached, Sally instructed one of these to get ready for his bath.

"No," he replied, bluntly.

Sally becomes more of the schoolmistress. "Go and get ready for your bath NOW."

"Shan't," comes the reply.

At this point Sally takes the offending child by the scruff of his neck, marches him upstairs, removes his clothes and dumps him in the bath.

By now there is a lot of screaming, and the sponge and duck are thrown.

So, Sally comes downstairs and instructs me to take over. Up I go and berate the offending child in quite forceful terms.

He is surprised and stops screaming. Then, speaking in quite a measured way, he says, "I think it would be better if you dealt with this when you are a bit calmer."

I have to admit that this took the wind out of my sails and caused me to wonder whether I might be losing my touch.

He then adds, "The trouble is, I hardly know you at all. You are a complete stranger."

Happily family responsibilities still allowed me the chance to resume my acting career. This began with the Rye Players and a performance of *Rebecca*, a dramatised version of the Du Maurier novel. Often dramatised versions of novels fail to work, and this was no exception. I played the part of Mr de Winter. At one point the stage instructions require me to carry the heroine up the stairs. This would have been physically impossible. The magistrate in the last act was played by the local printer who was elderly, forgetful and deaf. Every time he took a prompt, which was frequently, he stared at the prompt and shouted, "What?" It was disconcerting that even as I stood on stage, I could see people in the front row looking surreptitiously at their watches. A couple of my friends came to the production and declared that it was the funniest play they had ever seen.

From here I graduated to the Stonegate Amateur Dramatic Society which took things a lot more seriously.

My favourite role was that of Mr Condomine in *Blithe Spirit*. He is visited by the ghost of his first wife who berates him for all his failings, in particular taking her on honeymoon to Budleigh Salterton. It worried me that Budleigh Salterton was possibly preferable to Bulgaria.

However, Rwanda had somehow got under my skin and I did keep going back. Eventually I decided to set up a charity to develop the humanitarian work we had begun with the Church.

With wonderful support of my family and friends we set up a Board of Trustees and established Rwanda Aid.

At this point I had spent very nearly five years in Rwanda and I had learned to recognise some of the possible pitfalls: the Christmas debacle at the refugee camp spelt out the danger of handouts and we were determined to focus on building capacity so that gradually people could fend for themselves. I also had a better understanding of whom I could trust, at least so I thought.

One of the early tasks was to register the charity in Rwanda. I was pointed in a number of different directions to achieve this but eventually settled on the Office of Immigration. The primary purpose of this institution seems to be to teach people patience. Everywhere people are waiting.

I found a room which had INGO printed on the door and felt that this was promising. Happily, there was a man behind the counter so I cheerfully explained my purpose. He said nothing but pointed to a chair in the corner. I dutifully sat down and waited.

A couple of hours later he reappeared and beckoned me back to the counter. He produced a long list of requirements and explained that I had to meet these if I wanted to register the charity. It was a long list, and detailed. Requirements included O and A level certificates (originals, not copies), a letter from the Mayor, certified documents from Company House and the Charity Commission and my birth certificate – were they doubting that I was born?

I drew a deep breath. Fair enough. They wanted to be sure that we were not some fly-by-night organisation so off I went.

A few months later I returned with the task completed. I realise now that I might have made a tactical error at this point as I planted the completed booklet on the counter with a slight air of triumph. My official eyed it suspiciously and then shook his head saying that he could not accept it like that. He hadn't even opened it!

"What's wrong?" I enquired, trying to keep my voice steady.

"It's not stamped."

"We don't have a stamp."

"I can't accept it unstamped."

So off I went, had a stamp made and stamped each page with Rwanda Aid, failing to see what difference this made.

Back I went, waited an hour or two, and then presented the booklet again.

Again, it was rejected, unopened.

"What's wrong this time?" Disbelief.

"It's got the wrong binding."

"You mean that if I don't change the binding you will refuse to register the charity and I will have to pack up and go home."

"Yes. We didn't ask you to come here."

It took me months to produce a version that was acceptable.

At first I reacted with outrage, but gradually I realised there was a lesson to be learned. If we go to work in another country we must accept that we are guests and have to work with the authorities and under their rules and guidance.

This has helped to define our approach of working closely with the government to identify the main challenges and seek to work with them to find effective and acceptable solutions. We are to be junior partners, always embarking on projects with the target of gradually withdrawing our support to leave the Rwandans to run things for themselves.

The first manager we appointed was from the refugee camp. We had helped his family and even paid for him to complete his training in Kigali. He was a charming, well-presented young man with good managerial skills but sadly we learned that he was not to be trusted.

Initially I was outraged, but on reflection I am less inclined to pass judgement. Had I been through what this man and his family had suffered I would probably have had few scruples about taking what I could to make the future more secure.

P was our next manager and held the post for some years. He was a lay priest and had been the executive secretary of one of the sectors on Nkombo Island. He was a lovely man and a good manager, but he was often tired and I know that he slept badly, haunted by his experiences of the genocide as a schoolboy.

On one occasion he invited me to his sister's wedding. I declined on the grounds that these were usually extremely long affairs of which I understood very little. Anyway, I knew that the main reason he was asking me was so that I would allow him to use the RA vehicle.

The Monday after the wedding one of the other members of the Rwandan team told me that I should have been there. He was right. It had been more than a wedding.

Apparently at the height of the genocide many Tutsis had been rounded up in the stadium in Kamembe to be starved and slaughtered. Peter's father had gone to the stadium and bribed the guard to give him two of the children. He managed to smuggle two little girls back to his village, bribing the guards at each of the check points. The girls were carefully hidden and survived. Now twenty years later, they wanted to thank Peter's father by presenting him with two cows.

Once again, I reflected that even as the genocide demonstrated the depths of depravity to which humans could stoop, it also threw up many acts of outstanding humanity and heroism.

# Chapter 19

# Street Children

The experience of trying to register the charity seared in my mind, I was always conscious of the importance of working with our local authorities. This was not always easy. The local Mayor was busy and elusive. I always tried to make appointments but never had much faith in them. We would arrive at the appointed hour, explain our date with the Mayor to his personal assistant and be allocated seats in the waiting room. An hour or two would pass and we might enquire politely whether the Mayor had been delayed. "Oh no. He's at a conference in Uganda."

When we did eventually pin him down, one of the things he urged us to do was to help with the problem of street children. This accorded perfectly with our mission and we were more than happy to take it on.

A walk through the town would make you keenly aware of the problem, Scrawny children would stop you, stick out their hands and say, "Give me money." They lacked subtlety ...

The District's way of dealing with the problem was their transit centre. From time to time the children would be rounded up and bundled off to the centre for three months' correction, ignoring the fact that for the most part it was society that needed correcting, not the children.

Because of our involvement we were allowed to visit the transit centre. It was a dreadful place. It was located in a remote, rural area and fenced off with rusty corrugated iron sheets. Inside there was one brick building which housed all the inmates. These included vagrants, prostitutes and children from the age of six. There was no furniture in the building and there were no facilities. It was locked.

We were allowed to observe "wash time". This involved the inmates being lined up in rows outside the building on their knees, with guards standing over them with sticks and guns. Then in turn each row was allowed to cross the field to do their ablutions in the primitive washroom.

Our first move was to try to get to know the children on the street to build their confidence. We organised games of football, generally accompanied with a good meal. We took to asking the children what they would choose if we could grant them one wish. We expected them to say food, or a bed, or a better home. We were surprised that the vast majority said that they would like to go to school.

This project quickly gathered support and we decided to build our own transit centre just outside the town. The District gave us a wonderful site leading down to the lake and we decided initially to build four houses, each big enough to house seven children, along with washrooms, a refectory, offices and a classroom.

We decided to offer both residential and day care. Children would be provided with new clothes, good meals, recreational opportunities and counselling. The only condition we insisted upon was they must attend schooling or training. For most this was not a problem. There were no locks on the doors and they were free to leave, but they were told that if they left twice, they would probably not be allowed to return.

We recruited staff who were able to understand that we were not punishing these children but rather providing them with a safe, caring and loving environment in which they could build their self-esteem and develop their skills to enable them to lead full and independent lives.

At the same time we were committed to finding the children's familial homes wherever possible, supporting them with a view to the children returning home.

In the early years this project was remarkably successful, with over 80% of the children being successfully reintegrated in their homes and schools. The local district could see the effectiveness of what we were doing and were very appreciative and supportive, but sadly the national Government was not convinced.

Understandably the powers that be were concerned that residential institutions were in danger of giving the community and families an excuse for relinquishing their responsibilities. All orphanages were closed and then all residential care for street children.

The Rwandan Government tended to enact its decisions in one fell swoop which could be fairly catastrophic. For example, in 2010 it was decided that all children should be taught in the medium of English, this despite the fact that many teachers had no English. I guess the argument was that if you do things in stages they never get done.

So our lovely street children project was closed although that it was only a transit centre with most children ending up being cared for back in their homes and despite its record of success. Since its closure the numbers of street children in the area have increased dramatically and our new Mayor is now campaigning for the national Government to think again. We shall see.

In the meantime, we look back and celebrate some wonderful success stories. Here are a few in the words of the "children" themselves.

> M.
> *"I came on the street when I was losing a hope for a better future. My father was killed after the genocide against Tutsis and my mother died because of cancer. We were three children and then one died.*
> *As we had no one to look after us, we decided to go on the street hoping to find a better life. My life changed when Rwanda Aid took me from the street to Baho Neza Mwana. I was given better accommodation, meals, health and social care ... and sewing training.*
> *When I left the village, I promised not to disappoint or return to my old life. I am now proud of running a sewing workshop in Bugarama Sector. I think that my husband*

*would not be able to love and marry me if I had stayed on the street. I am now a mother and responsible for my family, and we are living in our own house. I always thank Rwanda Action for every support I received."*

J.
*"My name is J. I am 22-years-old. I was admitted in BNM in 2013 and reintegrated in my family in 2014. I lived on the street for 19 months. I was strongly beaten by the passers-by and the restaurant owners every time when I tried to collect food leftovers. I slept under gutter. I could spend the whole day with no food.*
*I was taken to BNM to live there and slept on a bed with a mattress. I was given water for bath, clothes and food. I was taken back to school and this academic year, I always come in the top three of my class."*

JM.
*"I am 24-years-old and I was admitted in BNM in 2015 in day programme. I had been on street for 6 months begging for food because my family lived in extreme vulnerability. I lived with my foolish mum who died later. We sometimes lived depending on the neighbours' food and clothing. It was so difficult to rent a house and sometimes, because when not paid, we were chased away by the landlord. I dropped out of school.*
*I am now a successful hairdresser: I am paid 60,000 per month and I have a new appointment in Kigali. I live independently and can now afford food easily and feed my siblings. I can now rent a house easily because I am a haircutter in Kamembe town. I have good bedding facilities. I can now pay mutuelle health insurance."*

# Chapter 20

# Disability

In my early days in Rwanda, I was asked to help a little girl called Alivera who suffered from epilepsy. She had no father and her mother had to work in the fields during the day so that she could feed the family. Alivera was left on her own and often she would fall into the fire when having a seizure. Her little body was badly burned and scarred.

We helped Alivera by providing medication and we also gave her a pig! However, she lived in a very remote village, so it was difficult to monitor her well-being. When we visited her sometime later, we were distressed to find that she was starving: she was sixteen-years-old and weighed just sixteen kilograms.

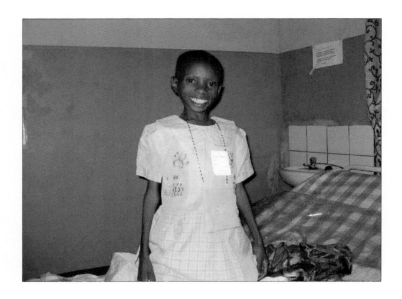

We took Alivera to our dispensary, but it was too late to save her: she was no longer able to eat. She knew that she was going to die, but she was a wonderful girl with not an ounce of self-pity: she liked to sing about the time when she would play her guitar in heaven.

There was little that we could do to help, but we did give Alivera a dress. She loved this. She would look in the mirror, and instead of seeing unwanted skin and bones, she saw a pretty girl.

After Alivera died, we decided to do what we could to prevent this happening to other children with disability.

Rather than starting from scratch we preferred to find a local project that had started work and therefore boasted some sort of track record. Our driver had just the answer and told us about a little group called "Ngwino Nawe" which means "Come to Us."

This was situated in a nearby village called Ntendezi so it was easy to visit. Strangely it was housed in a disused petrol station in some ramshackle huts behind the canopy. There were a dozen or so children with quite a range of disability and conditions were primitive.

What we liked, however, was that the three women caring for the children clearly did so for love rather than money.

We invested in this village so that it grew to accommodate over 80 children and we were delighted to see that increasingly they were successfully included and cared for in their homes and in mainstream schooling. When the founder, a feisty lady called Therese, died, we entered an agreement with the local district to develop the work with the aim of providing support for all children with disability in our area. We decided to call this "The Alivera Project" and gradually this has developed three units, the centre, the school and the village.

The Alivera Centre is a joy to visit. The needs of the children are many and varied, and in some cases quite acute, but the moment you come through the gate you sense a buzz of calm and constructive activity, and, above all, you know this is a happy place.

B really is a bit of a star. When we had our joint Board meeting with the District, he insisted on making his way round each member of the team giving him or her a great big hug and a few reassuring pats on the back. This was all the more remarkable knowing that when he joined the Centre the previous year B was completely unable to walk.

The local primary school is the Alivera school and is being developed as a School of Excellence for Special Needs and Social Inclusion – SESNSI. Most of the children from the centre graduate to the school and many pass successfully through it.

However, we then hit a barrier. Many of the disabled children battled through school against the odds and with immense courage and determination only to find that it was impossible to find employment at the end of it all. We felt that we were helping them along only to fail them at the last hurdle.

So we determined to address this by creating the Alivera Village.

The idea was to set up a series of shops and workshops, a farm and a restaurant, letting these out to local enterprise groups with a good track record of success on the condition that they took on an agreed number of apprentices with disability. These would be housed at the village for a maximum of two years and then be provided with seed funding to find employment outside the village or to set up on their own.

One of the first young people to arrive at the village was Jean Damascene. He is blind. He is in his late teens and has probably spent his entire life sitting in a darkened hut doing nothing. At most he will have been sent out to beg.

Jean's father brought him to the village and when Jean arrived, he was in some distress. This was all new and different and he was scared and tearful.

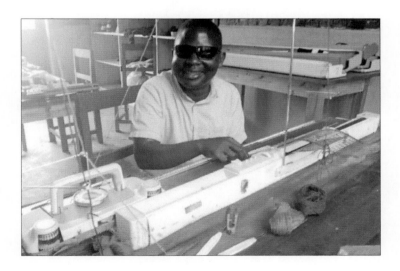

First, we showed him his room which he was to share with another young man with disability. When he discovered he had a bed he immediately brightened up, and he was encouraged to find other young people around him who faced similar challenges. However, it was when we took him to the knitting workshop where he was to work that he really changed. He discovered that his teacher was to be a lovely lady called Godberita and, like him, she was totally blind. Suddenly he saw a new world opening up in front of him, a world where there was future, a prospect of activity and independence. In a few short weeks the transformation in this young man was truly heart-warming.

Alina is deaf. She was only able to attend school with our support and the provision of a signer. A gutsy girl, she completed her primary school successfully, but then discovered that there were no employment opportunities for her. She returned home and spent six years doing nothing, rejected and unwanted. However, as soon as the Village was open, she was back and learning to make shoes.

We feel very privileged to be working with such brave and cheerful young people and we look forward to helping them to develop the skills that will enable them to lead full and independent lives.

At the same time, we hope that all those who visit the Village we begin to see for themselves that, with the right kind of support, people with disability are perfectly able to lead rich and productive lives.

# Chapter 21

# Education

Fundamental to the building, the capacity of the young is effective education: there is no better way of providing choice and opportunity.

Rwanda has been remarkably successful in registering most children for nine years relatively free education. However, sadly there is high dropout and high failure rate. The reasons for this are many and varied – poor resources, poorly paid teachers, the sudden switch to English as the medium for teaching and home poverty. However, our observation was that the main problem was the quality of the teaching.

This was all about filling pails rather than lighting fires. And what was worse was that the pails were often full of holes. Most teachers tended to march mechanically through the syllabus using endless chalk and talk and much rote learning. If they reached the end of the syllabus they considered their job, regardless of the fact that more than half the children had not understood what they had been taught.

We felt that it was vital to help teachers to challenge and inspire their pupils and to involve them more actively in the learning process.

We also felt it was important that the training programme should be a grass roots one working from the bottom up rather than the top down.

To initiate our programme we were immensely fortunate to find two young and extremely talented teachers who wanted to take on the challenge for a year. They agreed to work with us as volunteers in a remote village in the middle of Nyungwe Forest where educational standards and outcomes were as low as anywhere in the country.

It was a considerable challenge. They were to live in a small house with no electricity, no running water and no sanitation. The village was remote and had rarely been visited by a white person to the extent that the children would see one and burst into tears and run away.

It was hard. It was not so much that there were very few home comforts: what was more difficult was that they were under endless scrutiny. Like visitors from outer space.

But the two were made of stern stuff and persevered. Indeed, they were encouraged to find amongst some of the teachers a real enthusiasm to learn and develop.

As the year progressed, we felt it was really important to introduce the Rwanda Education Board to what we were trying to do. After much persuasion the official in charge of teacher training agreed to visit the village. He arrived in a bad mood. He had had no idea how remote the place was where we were working – three hours off the main road along a perilous and bumpy track – and he realised he would have to spend a night in the village without his creature comforts.

The next morning, he came to observe a lesson taught by one of the teachers our volunteers had been mentoring. It was to be a lesson on the human skeleton.

Normally a Rwandan teacher would conduct such a lesson as follows. He/she would arrive in the classroom scarcely acknowledging that there were fifty children packed like sardines, five or six to each rigid desk.

No. He/she would march straight to the blackboard at the front of the class and write "The Human Skeleton" at the top of the board, double underlined. He/she would then proceed to fill the entire board with information about the human skeleton which the children would copy laboriously into their books.

The lesson taught by the man from the Rwanda Education Board was very different. It was led by a Rwandan teacher whom our volunteers had mentored and trained. He was not a young man and had very definitely been set in his ways, so his transformation was all the more remarkable. I have to add that for some reason he conducted his entire lesson with his hat on.

He began the lesson in a surprising fashion. Instead of heading for the blackboard, he surveyed the fifty or so children in his class and asked them a question. "What is a human skeleton?" This had them thinking and coming up with some interesting suggestions.

He then instructed the class to form into six groups. They had clearly done this before as the groups were formed quickly and with no fuss.

He then instructed one member of each group to come to the front of the class and spend one minute looking at the labelled picture of a skeleton which he had prepared before the lesson. The child was then to return to his/her group and start drawing the skeleton whilst the second member came to look at the teacher's version. This carried on until all the member of each group had had their turn before the group skeletons were complete. The room was alive with the buzzing of children as they created their several skeletons.

Skeletons complete, each group was instructed to assess their neighbour's effort, a good bit of peer assessment.

The lesson then ended with twenty quick fire questions which the children answered so brilliantly the class was invited to finish with a celebratory dance.

It was a brilliant lesson by any standards.

The man from the Board watched it all wide-eyed: he had never seen anything like this before.

Then he shook his head. "No," he declared, "you can't teach like this."

"Why not?" we enquired politely.

"If you teach like this you will never complete the syllabus."

He left in a hurry but seemed quite happy for us to carry on, and carry on we did, rolling out our programme gradually through local, carefully trained school-based mentors. We realised that a fundamental change in approach could not be flown in from outside: it had to be gradually developed and nurtured from the inside.

We kept in touch with our friends at the Rwanda Education Board and when we were able to demonstrate that the pupils in the schools where we had developed our more learner centred approach were beginning to achieve better results, they began to take a keener interest.

We also decided to introduce a further element to our training. We wanted to engage the pupils, to excite their interest, but we also recognised that the pitching of lessons was really important.

As in our schools in UK, in Rwanda there is an awful lot of summative assessment, telling us how much the children do or don't know at the end of the process.

We have tried to switch the emphasis towards formative assessment carried out at the beginning of each year and helping the teachers more accurately to meet the needs of the children in their care.

The results are now so encouraging that the Rwanda Education Board is certainly sitting up and taking notice. Far fewer children are failing their important P6 examinations which do or do not qualify them for secondary education, and far more children are achieving success at the higher grades.

What's more, the atmosphere in our schools is changing. They are no longer places of drop-out and failure – pupils, parents and teachers are all enjoying the greater level of success. Fires are lit and there is dancing.

## Chapter 22

# Postscript

When I indicated my intention of going to work in Rwanda most of my family and friends were immensely supportive. However, there was the occasional critic. I remember one chap saying to me, "I hear you're planning to go out to Rwanda." When I replied cheerily that this was correct, he added, "Well, I think that is a complete waste of time. You'll not make any difference."

Twenty years on I can say with absolute confidence and conviction that he was wrong. I would go further and say that in partnership with our Rwandan team and with the support of the Rwandan government we have helped to make a difference to hundreds of thousands of lives. The stories that precede this chapter provide lots of examples of individual lives that have been transformed, but it goes further than that. When we opened the Alivera Centre and then the Alivera Village it was wonderful to see the Government both at local and national level, and the entire local community, taking huge pride in the initiative and achievement. Entirely without our prompting, a banner was strung across the road which said in Kinyarwanda, "WE MUST CARE FOR OUR CHILDREN WITH DISABILITY." Yes!

And in the afternoon, when we organised our very own Paralympics, the whole village turned out to support the children.

We were witnessing the beginning of a fundamental change in the understanding of disability and the Rwandan society's attitude towards it.

In the same way our innovative teacher training programme is beginning to achieve such remarkable improvements in the retention and performance of pupils that there is a very good chance that it will be adopted as part of the national programme bringing benefit to huge numbers of children.

I shall be forever grateful for the opportunity of working in Rwanda: it has been a wonderfully enriching experience.

In 2013 I learned that I was to be awarded an OBE. I did hesitate. Briefly. Order of the British Empire. Was that really what it had all been about? I was acutely aware of the "White Saviour" syndrome, and I had made a point of trying to ensure that the role of the UK team was supportive and enabling, with an exit strategy that would leave the Rwandans to develop and sustain the initiatives that we had jointly piloted together. This is why we changed the name of the charity from Rwanda Aid to Rwanda Action.

However, for someone as insecure as me, the award was irresistible. Receiving it from Prince William (his first go) was a wonderful moment, especially as my lovely wife and three children were able to be there for the occasion. I realise that I was receiving the award on behalf of all the many people who have made a success of the work in Rwanda, especially the team out there, but I did still feel proud. I think my dad would have been pleased, too.

Mind you, I was quickly put in my place after the ceremony. Custom has it that photographs are taken in the courtyard in front of the palace. There were three Gurkha soldiers present who had received awards for bravery. One of them approached and asked, "Please may we take photograph." I was immensely flattered and started to straighten my tie and ensure that my hair was in order. The soldier then realised that I had misunderstood him. "No, no," he explained, "Photograph of your son." (He's a pop star)

To a certain extent. I have become more confident, and I have learned things. I have come to dislike the complacency and self-satisfaction that sometimes come with wealth and status. They are as unattractive as envy is in those who are less well off. If we are privileged, we are privileged to serve, and if we are disadvantaged, we should surely try to have the aspiration and determination to do better for ourselves.

I have also learned that excess has a greater potential to damage the human soul than deprivation.

I would never wish to romanticise poverty: I have seen extreme poverty and it is destructive and terrible.

And yet ...

Early on the *Daily Telegraph* made us one of their Christmas charities. They sent a wonderful Features Editor called Alice Thomson to write a series of articles in the lead-up to Christmas. This she did brilliantly.

At the time, Alice had a young family, so she was particularly interested in the children. One day we travelled to a remote village through the forest. It was a good three hours along a very bumpy track. As we arrived hundreds of children emerged from the bushes. They were in rags, had spindly legs and distended tummies and were very dirty. And Alice turned to me and said, with some surprise, "But, David, they all look so happy."

Later the then editor of the *Telegraph*, Charles Moore, did a follow-up visit, and afterwards he wrote these wise words:

"A Westerner is confronted by the paradox that the very ills he is trying to relieve in Africa somehow give the people there something that he lacks. It is not that poverty and disease are good: it is that they confront people with the difference between what matters and what doesn't."

I think that is true and I also think that I now have a slightly better grasp of what matters and what does not.

The ghosts still haunt me. They haunt me in my dreams. Here I am trying to reach a class of children who are about to sit their exams knowing that I have failed to teach them all year, just haven't turned up. The way to the classroom is strewn with rocks and ravines, and in my panic, I am frozen in agonising slow motion.

Or now I am desperately trying to explain the complexities of a text to a class, or regale a large audience with the wonders of what we are achieving in Rwanda, and my voice is so hoarse that I can barely muster a whisper.

However, there remains real and important consolation: although we may never be able entirely to shake off the influences of our youth, I do know now that we do not have to be defined or imprisoned by them.

EIN HERZ FÜR AUTOREN A HEART FOR AUTHORS À L'ÉCOUTE DES AUTEURS MIA ΚΑΡΔΙΑ ΓΙΑ ΣΥΓ
HJÄRTA FÖR FÖRFATTARE UN CORAZÓN POR LOS AUTORES YAZARLARIMIZA GÖNÜL VERELIM S
CUORE PER AUTORI ET HJERTE FOR FORFATTERE EEN HART VOOR SCHRIJVERS TEMOS OS AU
SZÍVÜNKÉRT SERCE DLA AUTORÓW EIN HERZ FÜR AUTOREN A HEART FOR AUTHORS À L'ÉCO
CORAÇÃO BCEЙ ДУШОЙ К АВТОРАМ ETT HJÄRTA FÖR FÖRFATTARE Á LA ESCUCHA DE LOS AUT
AUTEURS MIA ΚΑΡΔΙΑ ΓΙΑ ΣΥΓΓΡΑΦΕΙΣ UN CUORE PER AUTORI ET HJERTE FOR FORFATTERE EE
YAZARLARIMIZA GÖNÜL VERELIM SZÍVÜNKÉRT SERCE DLA AUTORÓW EIN HERZ F
VOOR SCHRIJVERS TEMOS OS AUTORES CORAÇÃO BCEЙ ДУШОЙ К АВТОРАМ ETT HJÄRTA F

# The author

David Charles Chaplin was born in the city of
Norwich in 1947, the youngest of six children.
Can Do Better is his first book, a memoir of his
life and times working in Rwanda. In his own
words, he had an undistinguished school career,
attending both Town Close House and Leys School,
Cambridge before going on to earn a degree in
English from Durham University. After teaching at
a number of secondary schools for seven years, he
was appointed head teacher of Vinehall School,
Robertsbridge, East Sussex, serving in the role for
twenty-five years. After taking early retirement,
he founded Rwanda Action in 2008 and served
as Chief Executive Officer for fourteen years. He
was awarded an OBE for services to the Republic
of Rwanda in 2013. A father of three, he enjoys
acting, theatre, golf and public speaking, and now
lives in the village of Peasmarsh, East Sussex.

Printed in Great Britain
by Amazon

32394874R00071